FABIAN SOCIETY

C000081960

The Fabian Society is Britain's leading left of centre think tank and political society, committed to creating the political ideas and policy debates which can shape the future of progressive politics.

With over 300 Fabian MPs, MEPs, Peers, MSPs and AMs, the Society plays an unparalleled role in linking the ability to influence policy debates at the highest level with vigorous grassroots debate among our growing membership of over 7000 people, 70 local branches meeting regularly throughout Britain and a vibrant Young Fabian section, and the Fabian Women's Network. Fabian publications, events and ideas therefore reach and influence a wider audience than those of any comparable think tank. The Society is unique among think tanks in being a thriving, democratically-constituted membership organisation, affiliated to the Labour Party but organisationally and editorially independent.

For over 120 years Fabians have been central to every important renewal and revision of left of centre thinking. The Fabian commitment to open and participatory debate is as important today as ever before as we explore the ideas, politics and policies which will define the next generation of progressive politics in Britain, Europe and around the world.

Fabian Society
11 Dartmouth Street
London SW1H 9BN
www.fabians.org.uk

Fabian Ideas 630

First published 2011
ISBN 978 0 7163 0630 6

Series Editor and Editorial Director: Tom Hampson
Editorial Manager: Ed Wallis

British Library Cataloguing in Publication data. A catalogue
record for this book is available from the British Library.

Printed and bound by DG3, London, UK

To find out more about the Fabian Society, the Young
Fabians, the Fabian Women's Network and our local
societies, please visit our web site at **www.fabians.org.uk**.

Punishment and Reform

How our justice system can help cut crime

Edited by Sadiq Khan MP

With chapters from Lord Victor Adebowale,
Baroness Jean Corston, Shauneen Lambe, Paul McDowell,
Kevin McGrath, Barry Mizen, Dame Helen Reeves,
Professor Robert Reiner, Professor Julian V Roberts,
Matthew Ryder QC, Lord Norman Warner, Phil Wheatley CB

About the authors

Rt Hon Sadiq Khan MP is the MP for Tooting. Since October 2010 he has been the Shadow Lord Chancellor and Shadow Secretary of State for Justice. He has previously been a Minister in the Department for Communities and Local Government and Minister of State for Transport. Before becoming an MP he was one of the country's leading solicitors and an elected councillor in Wandsworth for 12 years. He is a former Chair of the Fabian Society and a member of the Fabian Executive Committee.

Lord Victor Adebowale has been Chief Executive of Turning Point since 2001 and has more than 25 years experience in the health, social care and housing sector. In 2000, Victor was awarded the CBE for services to the New Deal, the unemployed and homeless young people. He was appointed as a cross bench peer in 2001.

Baroness Jean Corston was Labour MP for Bristol East until 2005. As an MP, she was the first woman elected to chair the Parliamentary Labour Party. Her review into vulnerable women in the criminal justice system was published in March 2007 and outlines "the need for a distinct radically different, visibly-led, strategic, proportionate, holistic, woman-centred, integrated approach".

Shauneen Lambe is the Director of Just for Kids Law. She is an attorney in Louisiana and a barrister in UK. She started her career working for Clive Stafford Smith representing people facing the death penalty in the USA. In 1999 she helped establish the charity Reprieve. In 2006 she set up Just for Kids Law providing support, advice and representation to young people in London.

Paul McDowell is Chief Executive of Nacro, the leading crime reduction charity in England and Wales. He previously enjoyed a 20 year career in the Prison Service culminating in spells as Governor of HMP Coldingley and then HMP Brixton. He also spent a year seconded to the Home Office working in the Prison Minister's Private Office.

Kevin McGrath is Senior Adviser to F&C REIT Asset Management. He is Chair of the McGrath Charitable Trust; Trustee of Howard League for Penal reform; The Clink Restaurant Charity; The National Education Trust; and The WAVE Trust. He is an Ambassador for the Make Justice Work Charity and served as an Commissioner on the Independent Commission on English Prisons Today.

Barry Mizen and his wife Margaret, together with the rest of their family, set up the Jimmy Mizen Foundation following the murder of their son in May 2008. The foundation works to promote the good in young people. One strand of this is called the Awareness Project and much of their time is now spent visiting schools and prisons. See www.jimmymizen.org for more details.

Dame Helen Reeves was the founding Chief Executive of Victim Support and the Witness Service in the UK, retiring in 2005 after 26 years with the charity. Previously she had served for 12 years in the Probation Service. She was also a founding member of Victim Support Europe, serving both as Secretary and Chair.

Professor Robert Reiner is Professor of Criminology, Law Department, LSE. His most recent books are: 'Law and Order: An Honest Citizen's Guide to Crime and Control' (Polity Press 2007); 'The Politics of the Police' 4th.ed. (Oxford University Press 2010); 'Policing, Popular Culture and Political Economy: Towards a Social Democratic Criminology' (Ashgate 2011).

Professor Julian V Roberts is Professor of Criminology in the Faculty of Law, University of Oxford. He is Editor of the European Journal of Criminology and has been a Visiting Scholar in the Department of Justice Canada, a Visiting Professor at the Catholic University of Leuven and Visiting International Professor, Faculty of Law, Université Libre de Bruxelles.

Matthew Ryder QC specialises in complex crime and its interplay with civil law, including judicial review, police law, and claims under the Human Rights Act. He sits as a Crown Court Recorder and was one of only three Silks appointed in 2010 with expertise in both civil and criminal law.

Lord Norman Warner is a Labour member of the House of Lords. He was Senior Policy Adviser to Jack Straw when he was the Home Secretary from 1997 to 2001. He was a member of the Dilnot Commission on funding of care and support. He was the first Chair of the Youth Justice Board and was a Minister of State at the Department of Health from the summer of 2003 until December 2006.

Phil Wheatley CB is a former Director-General of the National Offender Management Service and before that he was Director-General of HM Prison Service where he was the first Director-General to have previously been a prison officer. He retired in 2010.

CONTENTS

REHABILITATION AND RELEASE

CRIME AND SOCIETY

Acknowledgements

In the spirit of joined up policy making, this has been a collaborative project with experts, influencers and practitioners from across the justice sector. I thank the authors of this pamphlet not only for their chapters, but their engagement, ideas and encouragement which have made editing it an informative and thought provoking experience.

I would like to thank the following for their time, hard work and contributions:

Lord Victor Adebowale, Baroness Jean Corston, Shauneen Lambe, Paul McDowell, Kevin Mcgrath, Barry Mizen, Dame Helen Reeves, Professor Robert Reiner, Professor Julian V Roberts, Matthew Ryder QC, Lord Norman Warner and Phil Wheatley.

Sunder Katwala, the previous General Secretary of the Fabian Society and Andrew Harrop, the General Secretary of the Fabian Society, have both provided valuable support for this project, as have Tom Hampson and Ed Wallis in helping bring this pamphlet to fruition.

My Political Advisers Dr Nick Bowes and Leah Kreitzman deserve great thanks for their insights and assistance, both in the production of this pamphlet and their support generally.

The Barrow Cadbury Fund has kindly provided financial backing to the project and everyone involved is grateful for their generous support.

I hope that this pamphlet proves to be a useful resource in the important debates about how we can make our justice system work effectively to cut crime, improve the experience of victims and witnesses as well as punishing and reforming offenders.

I look forward to discussing the ideas presented here with fellow Fabians and others in the months ahead.

As ever, I would like to thank my wife, Saadiya, and my daughters, Anisah and Ammarah, for their patience and understanding.

Introduction

Sadiq Khan MP

Crime fell by 43 per cent over Labour's last period in government. There were several reasons for this, but they were all underpinned by an approach that was tough on crime and tough on its causes. This record is something I am proud of, and as we develop our programme for government ahead of the next election, it is a legacy on which I seek to build.

Reducing crime is still the overriding priority. I grew up on a council estate in the south London constituency I now have the immense privilege to represent in parliament. I know from experience that victims and offenders often live side by side. The fear that my bike may be nicked or my brothers and sister mugged by other local people was just a way of life. And it is a way of life that, despite huge reductions in crime, is all too common for many people in communities up and down our country. There's a real risk that with cuts to frontline police and criminal justice services, this feeling will become yet more common still.

Crime is not just something an offender inflicts on a victim; it creates social volatility that affects everyone. It damages communities and society as a whole. Battling the scourge of crime and anti-social behaviour is one of the things that drew me to a career in the law and, later, parliament.

As a solicitor, I spent considerable time with clients and their families, with victims and witnesses; in courts, in tribunals, in prisons; and I grappled with the intricacies of our justice system on a day-to-day basis. As an MP I see first hand the effects crime has on my constituents and over the last year, as Shadow Justice Secretary, I have met with and listened to the men and women working in the justice system trying to deliver, with limited means, its key objectives: to catch, convict, punish and reform offenders while protecting the public and supporting victims.

Victims should be at the heart of our justice system, not only because they deserve to be treated with respect and dignity, but also because their co-operation and trust is vital for it to function effectively and bring offenders to justice. But victims are often treated as mere bystanders as their cases proceed through the courts. They are too frequently kept in the dark about the details of a trial, access to court papers are often difficult to obtain and complex legal processes difficult to understand, all of which can and should be remedied quickly and at little cost. But when victims report that their encounter with the justice system was more traumatic than their encounter with the perpetrator of the crime against them, it is clear that a more significant shift in attitudes to and treatment of victims is required.

But alongside a justice system that protects and supports victims, we must have a penal system that successfully punishes and rehabilitates offenders. Many victims I have met express a sincere hope that, once the perpetrator of their crime has been brought to justice, work can be done to ensure that they don't reoffend and other people don't suffer in the way they did. We owe it to these victims to do what we can to ensure others don't have to go through the same trauma they have had to endure – by reforming criminals before they complete their sentences.

It is right that people who commit offences are properly punished, either by having their liberty removed with a custodial sentence or through a tough community order. Punishment is a fundamental part of our justice system and one that is central to maintaining public trust and confidence in it and preventing people taking the law into their own hands. Those who commit serious and violent offences should be incapacitated in prison for a long time, and released only when they no longer pose a threat to the public. But the majority of people in our prisons today will be out within the next ten years and so, for the sake of our communities, we have to try to stop them reoffending by rehabilitating them.

Alongside a justice system that protects and supports victims, we must have a penal system that successfully punishes and rehabilitates offenders

Our prisons are full of people who are illiterate and innumerate, who suffer from multiple mental health problems and drug addiction, who were in care as children and excluded from school. So I am under no illusions about the scale of the rehabilitation challenge. Dealing with the underlying issues many offenders face so they can get a job, reconnect with family and find a home upon release – all essential to successful rehabilitation – requires a concerted, cohesive approach. Though the last Labour government made some progress in bringing down reoffending rates in recent years – by investing in probation, prison health care, trying to pursue a joined up integrated approach to offender management programmes, exploring the benefits of restorative justice and much more – they remain stubbornly high. 49 per cent of convicted prisoners are reconvicted within a year of release, with unknown numbers committing offences that don't lead to a conviction. 61 per cent of prisoners who have served a sentence of less than 12 months are reconvicted within a year of release, and for prolific offenders who have served more than 10 custodial sentences the reoffending rate is a staggering 79 per cent.

Driving down these statistics by providing drug and alcohol treatment, education, skills training and resettlement back into the community – with all that entails – could effectively bring down the financial cost to the country, estimated at £11bn annually for youth offending alone, and the untold cost of human misery repeat offenders cause.

Focusing on these issues will mean fewer people committing crime. And this should be the test of this – or any – Government's policies. My fear is this Government will fail the test because its focus isn't on cutting crime – it's on cutting costs. For all the talk by the Ministry of Justice of ushering in a new approach to rehabilitation, it is simultaneously slashing a quarter from its budget. And it is frontline jobs in the prison and probation service that will be lost because of these cuts.

Of course, I agree that rehabilitation is a key component of fewer people committing crime. It's in all our best interests, particularly the victims of crime and the communities that criminals blight. But the consequences to public protection of a combination of the scale and pace of the cuts could be severe. Letting people out of prison without the professional support required to oversee their successful rehabilitation is taking an unjustifiable risk with public safety.

In the current economic climate, tough decisions have to be made and savings need to be found, but this shouldn't be to the long-term detriment of our prison estate, probation service and the public they protect. Our job is to find out what's the best and most cost effective passage for an offender through the criminal justice system that ensures their rehabilitation, in a way that shows justice is served, victims are supported and protected, and the system works to help bring down crime.

I am leading a working group of experts from across the criminal justice field to help answer these questions and formulate a policy programme that strikes the right balance between punishment and reform. This pamphlet will inform that review. And while nothing by these independent authors forms Labour Party policy, the challenges and solutions they elucidate are informative and thought provoking, will add to the much needed debate on reforming the criminal justice system and deserve serious consideration.

While nothing by these independent authors forms Labour Party policy, the challenges and solutions they elucidate are informative and thought provoking

I want to focus on how we support victims, show justice has been done, appropriately punish offenders, and successfully rehabilitate them. To do this, we have to assess all aspects of the justice system, from conviction to release, as well as the political context in which the justice system operates and how it is perceived.

The causes of crime and why some people walk a criminal path while others follow the straight and narrow are of course complex and varied, but understanding them is crucial if we are to bring crime levels down and ease the burden on our justice system. Explaining the reasons for criminal behaviour is of course not to excuse it. Professor Rob Reiner gives his opinion that understanding the causes is a precondition to preventing crime. As Professor Reiner says, social injustice can provide the backdrop in which crime can flourish, but I believe it's important to understand that individual responsibility also has a big role to play.

As well as understanding causes, policy makers need to be in touch with public opinion on criminal justice. But Professor Julian V Roberts explains that the public's views on criminal justice are complex and if we want to see reduced levels of crime, it is up to politicians to lead the public in understanding what works, rather than simply following opinion polls.

However, a view held by the vast majority of the public, even those fortunate enough not to have experienced the workings of the justice system – and one which I strongly share – is that there needs to be greater consideration and respect for victims. I have committed Labour to enacting a new Victims' Law, as proposed by the first Victims and Witnesses Commissioner, Louise Casey, which will enshrine the proper treatment, information and rights bereaved families of victims of crime should receive. Louise Casey's position was informed by families of victims of murder and manslaughter and their experiences of the criminal justice system. One of those families was the Mizens, who tragically lost their son and brother, Jimmy, in a brutal attack in his own neighbourhood over three years ago. Jimmy's family have, since his untimely death, been working towards a safer community for young people in London and here Jimmy's father, Barry Mizen, explains how the legacy of his son will be one of peace and hope for young people.

It is clear that further work is required to ensure that all victims of crime, even the seemingly less serious offences, receive the necessary support and that the judiciary are sensitive to their needs. The founding Chief Executive of Victim Support, Dame Helen Reeves, explains why only clear political leadership will bring about the necessary changes to ensure that victims of crime don't feel victimised further by the criminal justice process.

But honouring the rights of victims does not have to come at the price of diminishing the constitutional rights of defendants to a fair trial. It is not a zero-sum game – protecting both victim and offender rights are necessary for the effective functioning of our courts. As Matthew Ryder QC points out, justice doesn't come from securing one set of rights over another. This is compatible with showing greater respect for the victim's position and feelings than they currently receive.

Once a trial is complete and a sentenced passed down, what's the best way to mange an offender in the justice system? Phil Wheatley draws on his 40 year career in the prison service to explain why we need a long-term and stable approach to prison policy if we are to make most effective use of taxpayers' money. However, answering the question requires a radical shift in the way our prison service is run, according to Lord Norman Warner, who draws on the successes we've seen in youth justice to argue that a disaggregated approach to the prison population, focusing on the different needs of different groups of offenders, is necessary if we are to make prisons work better to reduce crime. Baroness Jean Corston, following her seminal work on women in the criminal justice system, explains the success of non-custodial options for female offenders, while Lord Victor Adebowale highlights the intractable challenge of substance misuse in our prisons, which he thinks we should at least seek to mitigate even if we can't wholly overcome them.

It is not just drug and alcohol problems that form a roadblock on the path to rehabilitation for offenders. Illiteracy and innumeracy make getting offenders fit for a productive life outside prison difficult. I asked Paul McDowell, Chief Executive of the leading crime reduction charity dealing with offenders, NACRO, to consider how we can best achieve improvement in what I call the '4 R's' – reading, writing, 'rithmetic and rehabilitation. It is often at a very young age where these problems start and so we need to detect and deal with them before they escalate. Prevention and education initiatives, such as Sure Start, Family Intervention Projects and the Education Maintenance Allowance were starting to bear fruit and we saw reductions in youth offending over the last parliament – which is why it is so short-sighted to cut these schemes that have a proven track record of success. However, when prevention fails and young people do commit an offence, too often that sets them on an unbreakable cycle of crime and we see youth offenders seamlessly transition to adult offenders. Founder of the charity Just for Kids Law, Shauneen Lambe, speaks to a former young offender, 'FS', who has turned his life around, about how we can make the youth justice system more effective at responding to the unique needs of the children within it and reducing crime as a result. And, in his chapter, Kevin McGrath, himself a successful business owner, argues the importance of fostering a work ethic and creating opportunities for vocational training within prisons, so offenders are equipped with the skills they need to find employment on release and reduce the chance of further offending.

So, from prevention to charge, trial and conviction, sentencing options and the management of our prison estate, to release and resettlement in the community, people working in and affected by the justice system offer their views in the following pages on what changes could be made so justice is served more effectively in our country. I do not agree with all the analysis or that all the suggested solutions to the problems our justice system faces are necessarily the right ones, but I know that without the debates these pieces will incite, we won't find the ones that are. Now is the time to do the deep thinking and heavy lifting to achieve the right balance between deterrent, punishment and rehabilitation and to create a justice system the ensures crime levels are lower and communities are safer; and one in which the cycle of re-offending is broken.

VICTIMS AND OFFENDERS

1. BUILDING A LEGACY OF PEACE

Barry Mizen

On May 10th 2008, the day after his 16th birthday, Jimmy Mizen visited a bakery near his home in Lee, South East London, where he was murdered by another local teenager in a brutal and unprovoked attack. Since then, his parents, Barry and Margaret Mizen, and their family have been working towards a safer community for young people in South London and across the capital through the Jimmy Mizen Foundation. Here, Barry explains why the legacy of his son's tragic death has to be one of peace.

It is impossible for a parent to prepare for the emotion you feel when you lose a child. There is no single right way to deal with the grief. It can be all-consuming and, after more than three years, it is still gut wrenching in a way that is at times physically painful. Just as each child that has been lost to violence on our streets is unique, so is the way grief is felt by the family members they leave behind. No one hands you a manual of how to cope and everyone's experience is different. When our family lost our beloved son Jimmy, it changed our lives irrevocably.

All our relationships have changed to some degree as we've each tried to adjust. But we know we have to support each other or we would all individually fall apart. We are determined not to let what happened to Jimmy do any more damage to our family and that a positive impact on the lives of other young people would be the legacy of our son's death.

We decided that if we could channel our energies into assisting young people in our community we could help to make the sentiment many bereaved families share into a reality – that we will not be beaten by what happened and something good must come from it.

We were exposed to the machinery of our criminal justice system – an experience that thankfully very few families will ever have to bear. Rightly, due process has to be followed for both the defendant and the victim, so the process can be long, complicated for people without a legal background and very difficult. The perpetrator of Jimmy's murder, another local teenager with a history of bullying and destructive behaviour, was convicted and given a life sentence, with a minimum tariff of 14 years. For us, getting justice for Jimmy was not just about punishment for his killer, it was about finding and exposing the truth of what happened to our son.

In the immediate aftermath of Jimmy's death we needed answers about what had happened and how, and about who was responsible and what would happen to them. These were questions for the authorities – for the police, the lawyers, and the courts. But we soon began asking deeper questions that no Government or public body could answer alone: what has gone so wrong that young people are killing each other on our streets? What can we do to ensure young people don't resort to violence against each other? What sort of values should govern our society and how do we ensure they are instilled in all our young people? How can we stop a child born today from becoming a violent adult? Working towards finding answers to these questions is what we've been trying to do since Jimmy's death.

Not long after Jimmy died, my wife Margaret and I were invited to a local school by the chaplain to talk to the pupils about what had happened as part of their citizenship education. Speaking to the schoolchildren and hearing their reaction made it clear to us that our experience must not be wasted – we realised that our Jimmy's story had such an impact and that it should be shared. This meeting, at a school in Bermondsey, really represents the beginning of what was to become the Jimmy Mizen Foundation.

The ethos of the Foundation is that we all, each one of us, have to work together and play our part for a more civil, safe society. The aim of the Foundation is to foster participation of young people as responsible citizens in their communities, building awareness about the consequences when there's a breakdown of respect and an abdication of responsibility and to create relationships in our community so there is a sense of collective responsibility for each other and the area in which we live.

We knew that if we were to create a community that is safe for all our children, then they needed to be part of the conversation on how we all achieve it. Speaking to children about our experience and hearing their's is incredibly valuable. We have worked with groups of schoolchildren of all different ages and developed a presentation that gives details of what happened to Jimmy and why it's so important that there is a peaceful and considered response to crimes of the sort that he suffered.

It became quite clear to us that if young people feel that they have a stake in their local community they will feel some responsibility for it and how it functions. Given the right guidance and opportunity, young people who may have been vulnerable to falling into crime can be diverted from it. We had seen first hand how the Scouts can provide engagement and guidance for young people as Jimmy had been an active member and so we worked with them to improve our local area. We fundraised for minibuses to enable young people to participate in the Scouts' activities. We now have four 'Jimmy Buses' that are used by the youth and other local community organisations. To tackle the underlying issues of youth unemployment we've established an apprenticeship scheme in Jimmy's memory for people from South East London aged between 18 and 24 and are hoping to extend it, and develop a work experience program with businesses that want to give something back to the community.

My family has opened a coffee shop in Jimmy's memory, and a headquarters for the Foundation next door to it, near our home in Lewisham. The Cafe of Good Hope, run by Jimmy's brothers, isn't only a tribute to our son and a fundraiser for the work of the Foundation, it is also a safe haven for anyone who feels under threat or intimidated on the streets. From our discussions in schools, and with other groups of young people, it was worrying to discover how many felt a real fear of crime.

The outpouring of sympathy and love that we received from members of our community after Jimmy's death gave us hope that people did care about their neighbours and the security of the place where they live and they did want to work to make it better. There seemed to be a collective feeling that if communities look out for each other, keep an eye on our streets, know who local residents are and that there is somewhere safe for them, we can rebuild the ties that make our communities safer. That's what the broad-based community organisation, London Citizens, has tapped into and we've worked with them to develop City Safe Havens – sanctuaries for people if they feel unsafe on the street. We have established more than 200 across London and are working to roll them out in other parts of the country.

I think that the fact that Jimmy's murderer, Jake Fahri, although a known thug, was also a young member of our community demonstrated to people that all young people, not just our own children, are in some way our responsibility. After Jake killed Jimmy many people, including the press, were suddenly very interested in how he was going to spend the next two decades of his life, but I can't help thinking that if we'd shown the same level of interest in how he spent the first two decades my son might still be alive.

That isn't to absolve him from responsibility for his crime. I have no problem with the fact that Jake is now serving a life sentence for what he did. But I am far more concerned about what comes out of prison than when it happens. Will it be the same angry, dysfunctional man or a reformed member of society?

I do not see the benefit of a criminal justice system which seeks only retribution for crimes and not to reform criminals.

If I believed that longer sentences served in harsher conditions worked to deter people from crime or reformed criminals I would be all in favour of that approach. But unfortunately it's much more complex than that. I have worked with the Forgiveness Project on workshops in prisons to give offenders the opportunity to address the harm they have caused to bereaved families like mine. The offenders I meet have often experienced problems at school, constant run-ins with authority and addictions to drugs and other substances. These are problems which have their roots in early childhood and it is at that time in peoples' lives that they need to be addressed.

I do not see the benefit of a criminal justice system which seeks only retribution for crimes and not to reform criminals. We need to ensure that when offenders leave prison they have changed and are able to play a productive part in society. Understanding that their crimes have consequences not only for their own lives but for the victims and their families too is, I believe, an important part of that process.

I am convinced that trying to foster more civility and humanity in all aspects of life – from schools, to the streets, to prisons – is the only way to counter the incivility and violence my son and too many others faced. It's time to have a grown up discussion about what role each of us, from politicians and the police, to ordinary members of the community, can play. That means challenging widely held assumptions and asking big questions about the kind of society we want to be. We hope that this is what the Foundation we established in our son's name will help facilitate in some way. And that's what Jimmy's legacy will be. Not one of anger, vengeance or fear, but one of hope and peace.

2. Victims at the Heart of the System?

Dame Helen Reeves

For victims of crime, the experience of the criminal justice system can be deeply traumatic – sometimes even more than the crime itself. Over the last few years there have been some real leaps forward in the ways victims are treated, says Helen Reeves, but without clearer political leadership the criminal justice system is unlikely to make the fundamental changes required to truly support, protect and reassure victims.

After generations in the political wilderness, victims of crime now feature prominently in the policy statements of all political parties. We are told, for example, that "victims will be at the heart of the justice system" or that the system will be "rebalanced in favour of victims". At first sight, this seems a welcome development but what does it actually mean in practice? And is the heart of the justice system where victims' needs can best be met?

Crime of course covers a wide range of events, from property offences to life-changing acts of violence. The people on the receiving end of these offences vary in their reactions and needs as well as in the levels of financial or personal support available to them. What most of us want in the aftermath of crime is reassurance that the offence will not be repeated, that our feelings will be understood and respected and that, where property has been lost or destroyed, we will be able to replace it.

Services, such as Victim Support and various crime-specific provisions, are available in the community to assist with these priorities although they are constrained by limited resources. In addition, victims who report a crime to the police also want to know what action is being taken and, when an arrest is made, they usually expect to be kept informed as to the outcome. But in three decades working with victims of crime I have rarely met a victim who wishes, as a priority, to have a central role in the criminal justice process.

If a crime does come to court – and only about five per cent do – victims may have to give evidence and, even if they are not required as witnesses, some wish to attend in order to observe the trial. It is here that new and serious problems can arise. From the 1980s, a significant body of research began to demonstrate that victims often felt neglected or even insulted by the court process. Their status as the person most affected by the crime did not appear to be acknowledged and there was no-one to meet them or to explain the proceedings. If they heard evidence or statements in mitigation which they knew to be incorrect, there was no-one to tell. When required as witnesses, victims often complained about feeling harassed and intimidated by the cross-examination. When cases were adjourned (all too frequent an occurrence) it seemed that everyone except the victim was consulted about convenient dates.

In short, victims were being caused further and unnecessary distress by behaviour they encountered in the court, some even reporting that the experience of the trial had been worse than the crime itself. This phenomenon has become known as secondary victimisation and it has been confirmed and documented in many countries in addition to the UK. Provisions for victims in the context of the criminal trial should therefore focus on the prevention of secondary victimisation by showing respect for their position and consideration for their feelings. There has been little evidence in research that victims were expecting a more active role in the prosecution of the offender.

The good news is that wide-ranging measures have now been agreed both nationally and in Europe aimed at improving awareness of the needs of victims among criminal justice professionals and making suitable provisions for both victims and witnesses before, during and after the trial. In the UK, the Witness Service, run by the charity Victim Support, has been working in the criminal courts for almost twenty years, providing support and information to all witnesses and to other victims who wish to attend. The Crown Prosecution Service has published a 'Pledge for Victims' with comprehensive provisions for the protection of their interests.

Political leadership is needed to ensure that the policies which have been agreed are fully implemented.

The national Code of Practice for Victims of Crime, a statutory instrument setting out the standards required of all criminal justice agencies has been in force since 2006. However, according to the recent report of the Victims' Commissioner on The Needs of Families Bereaved by Homicide it would appear that many of these provisions have not been implemented, even for the most distressing crimes. My own experience is that significant changes have occurred in the culture and practice of the courts but, in spite of the best intentions of most of the professions involved, performance is constrained by lack of both time and money.

Political leadership is needed to ensure that the policies which have been agreed are fully implemented in practice and that the necessary resources are made available as a priority. Instead, all too often, new proposals are announced which divert attention from the main task, often with little evidence of the need. Policy makers appear to prefer the introduction of new and original ideas rather than endorsing the provisions of previous administrations and making it their priority to see those measures come to fruition. Some of the new measures proposed in recent years, by politicians and other authorities, move well beyond the prevention of secondary victimisation and could result in the victim having a more active role in the criminal justice process.

For example, it has been suggested that some victims should be provided with their own lawyer in court. It is difficult to see where this would fit into the context of an adversarial process, possibly resulting in a third party in the trial. More importantly it would suggest that the responsibilities of the prosecutor, accepted in their Pledge, would become redundant. Provisions in the Pledge include protecting the victim from oppressive cross-examination, challenging assaults on their character, promoting communication during the trial and applying for compensation on their behalf. Having a third lawyer, paid for by public funds, would seem an expensive option if the same results could be achieved by a well trained and sufficiently resourced Crown Prosecution Service.

Some commentators suggest that an inquisitorial system of justice, as practiced in much of Europe, might be more responsive to victims' needs. Here, victims can opt to be formal parties and, while this ensures that they are kept informed, in practice, only a minority choose to be full parties and few can afford legal representation. Comparative research still shows that victims in the UK report higher levels of satisfaction with criminal justice than in most other

European countries and they are also more likely to receive financial compensation from the offender.

Turning to the sentencing process, the Victim Personal Statement has been introduced to provide victims and, in the case of homicide, their families with an opportunity to tell the court about their loss, their feelings and their needs but not their opinions regarding the outcome for the offender. Clearly information is needed if compensation is to be ordered from the offender or if the sentence is to incorporate any measures for the protection of the victim but to what extent should the effects of the crime be taken into account? Consideration of the effects have always been an element in sentencing but should this include the unpredictable psychological impact or the social position of the person involved? The Sentencing Council has, in October, released new guidelines which will be used in both the Crown Court and magistrates' courts stipulating that effects on burglary victims should play a more prominent role in sentencing, "beyond the economic implications of a burglary".

This raises some important questions as to the position of the victim in the sentencing process. Should a burglar receive a lighter sentence if the householder chooses to forgive or a harsher sentence if they were already emotionally vulnerable? Is the crime of manslaughter more serious if the victim leaves a loving family than if he has no-one to speak for him? There has already been a case of a young man dying in a car driven by a drunken family friend where the sentence was reduced following a plea by the bereaved family. Is it fair to the offender, or even to the family for the victim to have this level of responsibility?

The root of the question lies in the separation of criminal and civil justice, well established in the foundations of English law. Unlike civil infringements, criminal acts are regarded as being committed against the whole community and the state is responsible for their investigation and prosecution. Victims do not have the stressful and sometimes dangerous task of bringing their own cases to court. Seen in this way, the criminal justice process should itself be regarded as providing an essential service to victims of crime, protecting them from unwelcome and unfair responsibilities. How many of us would wish to see this responsibility returned? Instead, a truly victim-centred policy would concentrate on increasing provisions in the community where they are most needed as well as ensuring that the process of justice provides protection and reassurance rather than causing further distress.

3. Justice and Rights

Matthew Ryder QC

Criminal justice rights are often portrayed as serving only the interests of the offender or as part of a balanced compromise. Neither is the case, says Matthew Ryder: real justice doesn't come from securing one set of rights by reducing others.

Any meaningful discussion on formulating new criminal justice policy has to begin with understanding the fundamental rights that are engaged.

But if, like me, you have practiced in the criminal courts for many years, you become aware of how easy it is for that discussion to be polarised. For those working within the criminal justice system, the focus is often on the offender. Will he or she have a fair trial? What is the appropriate sentence? How will the system rehabilitate them? For those outside the process, or those who become part of it as victims of crime, the concerns may be very different: will being a witness cause a victim even more pain and anguish? Are people properly protected? Has there been a just outcome at the end of it all?

I was taught as a law student that our fundamental rights provide a framework that ensures justice and fairness. They did not develop accidentally or in the abstract. They arose precisely because they were the fundamental principles needed to control executive power and ensure that monarchs and governments acted properly in the interests of all their citizens. Any policy that does not understand and observe those well-established rights is doomed to fail; eventually, it will compromise those established principles and cause injustice.

In recent years we have also seen that the credibility of our Government depends on it understanding the importance of criminal justice rights. Those rights have a very long and noble tradition in the United Kingdom. They do not simply belong to our history – they are part of our identity as a modern nation. A Government that fails properly to respect and observe those rights risks acting outside its democratic mandate.

For many people the rights in question are obvious and familiar: habeas corpus, the right to a fair trial, the right to due process. But criminal justice rights are often mischaracterised. Sometimes they are portrayed as nothing more than measures to serve the interests of a defendant. At other times they are presented as a necessary balance or compromise of fairness, by permitting an individual's rights to be overshadowed by broader public interests. In truth, neither is correct: there is far more to take into account than the rights of a defendant; and good policy does not compromise or secure one set of rights by reducing others.

The interrelationship and importance of the relevant rights was powerfully restated by former Law Lord, Lord Steyn in 2000,[1] and was approved in a later case by the former Lord Chief Justice, Lord Bingham, in 2004:[2]

"The purpose of the criminal law is to permit everyone to go about their daily lives without fear of harm to person or property. And it is in the interests of everyone that serious crime should be effectively investigated and prosecuted. There must be fairness to all sides. In a criminal case this requires the court to consider the triangulation of interests. It involves taking into the account the position of the accused, the victim and his or her family, and the public."

Lord Steyn's phrase "the triangulation of interests" is important because it describes the interplay of the three different considerations that sit at the heart of all criminal justice policy. Although he did not use the term 'triangulation' in the way that it is often understood in the political context, in criminal justice triangulation contains many of the merits and dangers as it does in politics. Approached correctly, the triangulation of interests means that every policy is carefully positioned so that the fundamental rights of those affected are respected at all times.

Approached incorrectly, triangulation results in crude compromises which are not guided by principle and which view rights as obstacles that must be overcome. For that reason it is important for any policy to begin by understanding the purpose of those three 'triangulated' interests and to take the correct approach to each.

It is important to remember that a criminal trial is not a dispute between the victim and the defendant. It is an action by the state against an accused person.

Beginning with the rights of an accused, it is – and should be – the defendant who is the focus of a criminal trial. That does not mean that the criminal process should be designed to work purely for the best interests or for the convenience of the defendant; at times it should be the opposite: if he or she is guilty of an offence the trial process should result in conviction and sentence. Similarly, respecting the rights of an accused should not result in prosecutions being unduly difficult or excessively costly – a fair process includes fairness to the prosecution also. Nevertheless, underpinning everything is the importance of a fair trial for the accused. That right is absolute.

It cannot be breached because doing so would permit an unfair trial, which by definition is anathema to our legal tradition and unacceptable in all circumstances. The consequence of this principle is that if we cannot prosecute fairly, we must not prosecute at all. But it also means that we should always seek to distinguish, with clarity, between those requirements that are truly critical to ensuring a fair trial and those which are not. The former can never be disregarded or compromised; the latter may be outweighed by competing considerations, but only if there are good reasons for doing so.

Second, in relation to the interests of victims, it is important to remember that a criminal trial is not a dispute between the victim and the defendant. It is an action by the state against an accused person. The state should provide an objective view of justice for those involved. A system that gives excessive weight to the desires of victims is as flawed as one which ignores them altogether. But understanding the 'triangulation of interests' means properly taking into account victims' positions even though they are not parties, not least because they are often the key witnesses. Have the victims been sufficiently informed of the relevant developments in the case? Is the prosecutor or court aware of the victims' views when making decisions that affect them? Is the process adequately protecting the victims, or simply putting them at even greater risk? Has the process resulted in fairness for the victims? Is justice for the victims better served by a sentence directed at retribution, or by one that focuses on rehabilitation? Unless those questions are in the minds of the public agencies involved, including the court, the legitimacy of the trial process will be fatally undermined.

Third, the public interest sits alongside the interests of the accused and the victim. Proper regard for the public interest ensures that we are aware of the wider implications of criminal justice policy beyond fair outcomes for the individuals. This may be as simple as guidelines that recommend the continuation of a prosecution even when both the perpetrator and the victim have decided not to co-operate with the police. Alternatively, respecting the public interest can involve much broader policy considerations that go beyond an individual case, such as the need for open justice and the media's ability to report on cases freely; the publication of reasons for controversial prosecutorial decisions; transparency in the appointment of judges; the preservation of the jury system; or even whether some powers afforded to the police and security services are inadequate or too broad.

The impact of these three distinct but connected interests is not merely theoretical. My professional experience of the Courts began first as a solicitors' clerk, then as a barrister, and more recently as Queen's counsel and a Recorder of the Crown Court. So, like all criminal justice professionals, I have had to engage in the difficult exercise of understanding how different interests intertwine. The family of a defendant may also be the neighbour of a victim, in a community where the public interest requires fair and effective criminal justice policy that makes a long term difference. Similarly, choosing the right sentence means not only punishing the offender, but also doing justice for the victim, and ensuring that the public have confidence that the likelihood of a convicted person reoffending is reduced. The three interests - defendant, victim, public - are inseparable. Any meaningful approach to new policy needs to take them all into account.

Some well known cases of recent years illustrate how our system has approached the 'triangulation of interests' highlighted by Lord Steyn and Lord Bingham.

In the case of **TB v The Combined Court at Stafford,**[3] the High Court was concerned with the tension between a victim's right to privacy and a defendant's right to a fair trial. Criminal courts frequently granted defendants access to a victim's medical records. In many cases, such records were necessary for a defendant to challenge the victim properly. In other cases, the records were of little relevance and the defendant sought them in order to embarrass or humiliate the victim. The High Court found that a narrow focus on the defendant's wish to view those records was not the right approach. The criminal court should have considered the victim's Article 8 rights alongside the defendant's right to a fair trial. If, on close examination, the disclosure of medical records really had been necessary for the defendant to have a fair trial then, of course, they should have been disclosed. But if they were not, then the witness's Article 8 right to have her medical records kept private should not have been compromised without good reason. As a result of that case, both the practice of the criminal courts and the relevant statutory provisions changed. The Crown Court now considers very carefully any application from a defendant to view the medical records of a victim. In an appropriate case the Court will even hear representations from separate counsel appointed for the victim – a step that would have been inconceivable years ago.

In **R v Davis**[4] the House of Lords considered the widespread practice developing in serious criminal trials of hiding the identity of a witness from a defendant. The practice had been developed by the criminal courts on a case-by-case basis. It gave significant weight to the victims' interest and the public interest, and assisted the prosecution of offences in communities where victims were afraid to come forward. But the practice had gone too far and did not include sufficient measures to protect the accused's interest. The House of Lords found that the defendant's inability properly to test the evidence of key witnesses– a vital component of the right to a fair trial – meant that the process was unfair and called the entire practice into question. However, the Government's solution was not to react to the judgment by criticising it or simplistically abandoning the practice that judges had developed. Instead, for the first time, the practice was properly regulated by statute.[5] The new provisions took account of the House of Lords' criticisms, but introduced a clear framework for protecting witnesses and the public interest while preserving the right to a fair trial.

The case of **S and Marper v the Chief Constable of South Yorkshire**[6] concerned police powers for the purposes of detecting crime. After a controversial case, the Government had introduced primary legislation that permitted the police to retain the DNA and fingerprints of all arrested persons, regardless of the seriousness of the suspected offence and whether or not the person was guilty of an offence. The measure plainly served the interests of victims by bringing to justice persons who might not otherwise have been identified. An accused person's interests were also protected – there was no suggestion that persons who had been identified by their DNA would not have a fair trial. But the policy failed properly to take into account the wider public interest that was affected. In due course the European Court of Human Rights found such a broad measure for the collection of genetic information was a disproportionate interference with the rights of the many thousands of innocent persons who, by virtue of being arrested, had their intimate biological data retained indefinitely by the Government.[7] As a result, a change of the legislation was necessary. The case of *Marper* is a good illustration of how criminal justice policy needs to be guided by a wider debate. At times even well-intentioned and effective crime prevention measures go further than the public interest is prepared to tolerate.

These three examples reveal one other important factor that prudent criminal justice policy should keep in mind. The task of understanding and observing the core rights that frame our criminal justice system belongs not only to the Government that formulates policy, but also to the legislature that enacts it and the judiciary that assesses it. When one branch of the state calls the other to account, or makes it clear that a policy or statutory provision has failed to respect the triangulation of interests, it is not a failure of the system but a success. It shows that the state is functioning properly as a whole in respecting the relevant rights. In doing so we will benefit from criminal justice policy that properly understands those rights and provides more considered, effective and progressive results.

Footnotes

1   *A-G's Reference (No. 3 of 1999)* [2001] 2 AC 91
2   *R v H; R v C* [2004] 2 AC 134
3   [2006] EWHC 1645 (Admin)
4   [2008] UKHL 36
5   Criminal Evidence (Witness Anonymity Act 2008)
6   [2004] UKHL 39
7   [2008] ECHR 1581

4. Prisons – Changing Direction

Lord Norman Warner

Here Norman Warner outlines a radical shift in the way the prison service and justice system could be run. He argues that politicians should design a more bespoke system that responds better to individual cases, and that local authorities could be given the budgets for prisons so they can buy in services for dealing with offenders in prison and serving community sentences.

During Labour's time in power, in a period of economic prosperity and falling crime, we have seen a rise of about 40 per cent in the prison population, with high rates of reoffending when people are released. Currently there are some 87,000 men, women and children in prison and the numbers continue to rise, particularly after the recent riots. Only among under-18s, where Labour reformed the youth justice system with more emphasis on community sentences and a dedicated independent body leading change, has there been a fall in the custodial population.

And there is little evidence that prison reduces crime much. Research by the Prime Minister's Strategy Unit in 2003 said that a 22 per cent increase in the prison population since 1997 had reduced crime by 5 per cent during a period when overall crime fell 30 per cent. It concluded that "there is no convincing evidence that further increases in the use of custody would significantly reduce crime". So prison doesn't really work but we continue to expand its use. What's more, we are now entering a period – possibly lengthy – when there will not be the public expenditure to continue as before.

Why has this happened? It is difficult to believe that over the huge increase in the prison population through the last 15 years is because Britain's population has suddenly become much more criminal, or that the police and CPS had become so efficient at catching and prosecuting them. Instead the facts suggest that we need to look for explanations and solutions in the areas of sentencing policy, the behaviour of the courts, the options available to them and the regimes in prisons. A few facts could be useful here.

- 70 per cent of the increase in demand for prison places between 1995 and 2005 is estimated to be due to changes in **custody rates and sentence length**.
- Over 36,000 sentences of up to three months were given by the courts in 2009. These **short sentences** result in prisoners having little prospect of being given effective programmes that might change their behaviour.
- The 2003 Criminal Justice Act fed **a huge unplanned rise** in the prison population through the indeterminate sentence of Imprisonment for Public Protection (IPP) and new high and mandatory starting points for those sentenced to life for murder and consequential tariff increases for all violent offences. By mid-2010 there were about 6000 IPP prisoners and less than 200 had been released. In 2001 the average total time in prison for a released murderer was 13 years but is now a minimum of 15 years and often more: the release rate for lifers has halved since 2007.

- The number of **women in prison** has increased faster than men in the last decade: by the end of 2010 there were over 4,200 women in prison. Jean Corston has set out the case for a "radically different approach" to women's offending.
- At the end of 2010 there were over 10,000 **young adults** aged 18-20 in prison, about 5 per cent more than the previous year. The under-18 custodial population had reduced by about 450 to just over 2000.
- Prison has a poor record for **reducing reoffending**. About 50 per cent of adults are reconvicted within a year of release. This rises to about 60 per cent for those serving sentences of less than 12 months: and to about 80 per cent for those with ten previous custodial sentences.
- **Community sentences** are 7 per cent more effective at reducing reoffending rates than custodial sentences of under 12 months.
- The proven potential of **restorative justice** both to reduce reoffending and improve victim satisfaction is significantly underexploited among the adult population.

Making prisons work better

The former Chief Inspector of Prisons, Dame Anne Owers, in her 2010 valedictory lecture, made it clear that in the past decade "there is no doubt that prisons became better places – better able to keep prisoners safe, provide a decent environment, offer some purposeful activity and provide some resettlement opportunities". Often, however, intended changes do not stick because there are too many people housed in prison, often for too short a time for it to work with them and often moved around too rapidly. About three-quarters of prisoners who have problems with both employment and accommodation on release reoffend within a year compared with just over 40 per cent of those without these problems.

If prisons are to work better, the population has to be reduced and that almost certainly means changing sentencing policy with a shift to more demanding community sentences and far fewer short and indeterminate custodial sentences. The upward creep in sentence tariff, particularly for non-violent offences probably needs review, with a stronger emphasis on proportionality and greater judge discretion. This is a subject for a separate paper. However to make sentencing change publicly and politically acceptable a great deal more thought needs to be given to the system changes needed both in prisons and the community. Here we need to draw on the lessons from Labour's successful youth justice reforms and the reports of Jean Corston on women offenders and Keith Bradley on mentally ill offenders. This will almost certainly mean changes to existing organisations such as the Prison Service and the National Offender Management Service (NOMS) as functions are redefined and reallocated.

Major lessons from the success of the youth justice changes were that to reform a dysfunctional system, (a) there had to be a strong focus on desired changes at central and local levels, (b) a wide range of agencies and organisations had to contribute to solutions rather than simply leaving matters to the criminal justice system, (c) new systems, organisational forms and leadership were required, and (d) changes had to be explained and marketed to courts for their behaviour to change. Relying on existing organisations was highly unlikely to produce change and existing organisations such as the probation and prison services were unenthusiastic about change.

As the Corston Report and the changes to the youth justice system have shown, offenders are not a homogenous group – and different groups have different needs. This a view that the prison service has often struggled to accept, preferring to have the flexibility to move prisoners round the system when there are population pressures. They have largely lost the argument with respect to juvenile offenders but it has taken a decade to achieve this and they opposed earlier efforts to apply the lessons of the youth justice system to 18-20 year-olds where there is considerable equivalence of need.

Politicians need to accept that we need to break down the offender population into separate categories, each with some commonality of needs, so that a more bespoke system of service responses can be designed around those needs. Without accepting that starting point it will be difficult to make progress towards radical reform. A provisional set of groupings could be:

- Youth justice up to 18
- Young adults, 18-20 or 18-24
- Women
- Seriously violent adult males requiring higher security
- Adult males
- Foreign prisoners who may be deported

It will be important to refine the definitions of these groups and to assess the relative merits and disadvantages of these categories, together with the relative priorities for separation. Trying to make all these changes in one go would almost certainly be a mistake; it has taken a decade for us to see the benefits resulting from the youth justice changes. The Corston report provides a strong basis for progressing more rapidly changes for women. The Coalition's proposed youth justice changes need to be reversed and consideration given to adding 18-20 year olds to the remit of the Youth Justice Board.

Local government and the community

A new policy dimension should be added to future offender policy and rehabilitation of offenders and that is the role of local government. Most offenders on community and short prison sentences – say up to three years – could reasonably be regarded as the responsibility of their home local authority. They are likely to go back to that area after prison and the local authority may well have to deal with their housing needs, a critical issue in rehabilitation. Local people will be more familiar with employment opportunities and skills development than staff in a more remote prison.

Local authorities are used to buying in services from a mixed economy of providers and have done this in social care, leisure services, refuse collection and social housing. These contracting skills are very much those needed for shifting the approach to changing offending behaviour. Tagging and curfews provide services that local authorities could buy in to restrict liberty as part of punishment, together with the organisation of payback schemes that YOTs have done for under-18s. It would be possible for local authorities to run weekend and evening custodial facilities with lower security costs than traditional prisons so that employment could be maintained, as happens in parts of Europe. Local authority participation in new Health and Wellbeing Boards would give them more leverage in ensuring the NHS played a fuller part in meeting the mental health and addiction needs of offenders.

There is no reason why local authorities – or consortia of them – should not be given the budgets for local prisons and those on community sentences to buy in the services required to meet the needs of the courts. The prison and probations services would be able to set up social enterprises to bid to provide service for these less serious offenders, along with service providers from the private, voluntary and social enterprise sectors.

For more serious offenders, where the security of the public was paramount, it would continue to be the responsibility of the Prison Service or approved private contractors to run the custodial services and mange the re-entry of released prisoners to society. It

Local authorities should play a much greater role in services for the less serious groups of offenders.

would be necessary for the overheads of the Prison Service to be reduced appropriately. It is difficult to see much of a role for NOMS after shifting much of the responsibility and budget to local authorities who would need to be compensated from these savings for their new management responsibilities.

Conclusions

In the current and foreseeable financial climate for public services the evidence suggests that it is poor value for tax-payers' s money to finance a prison population of 86,000 and rising. To downsize that population and improve rehabilitation sentencing policy for less serious offenders needs to change but so do the services and their organisation for underpinning a shift to more local and community-based punishments. Labour should learn from the success of its youth justice reforms and Jean Corston's report on women offenders in moving to designing services and their organisation around a new categorisation of offenders, as described above. Local authorities should play a much greater role in the organisation and purchasing of services for the less serious groups of offenders. Consideration should be given to a phased and orderly transfer of the budgets for funding these contracted servicesfrom NOMS and the Prison Service to local authorities or consortia of local authorities.

5. A Suitable Alternative?

Baroness Jean Corston

Jean Corston asks whether community alternatives would be better for female offenders. The results from women's community centres – usually run by women – are impressive. Helping women to learn new life skills and feel less like pariahs makes re-offending far less likely, she argues.

The prison population has just reached a staggering 87,000, but only around 5,000 of these are women. It's easy to see how women have become a neglected afterthought in justice policy.

But who are these women? When they arrive in prison, over 75 per cent of them exhibit some kind of psychological disturbance, compared with 15 per cent of the general female adult population. 75 per cent have taken an illicit drug during the six months before they enter prison; 58 per cent have used drugs daily. Half of them are alcoholics. They are generally poor and of low educational attainment. Yet only 3.2 per cent of them are considered a danger to the public – they are troubled rather than troublesome. They are mothers: about 16,000 children a year are affected by their mother's imprisonment. And it is generally petty crime that these women have committed – indeed, the coroner who conducted inquests into women who had taken their own lives while in Styal Prison in Cheshire, said they had committed "for the most part petty crime for whom imprisonment represented a disproportionate response". They are survivors of sexual and violent victimisation.

I recently heard of a woman who had committed over 90 shoplifting offences in the previous year; shocking until you learn that it was always for food for her children. Her well-off partner starved her of cash as a means of control, and her only income was child benefit.

Nearly three quarters of these women sentenced to custody are there for less than twelve months. And significantly, only 45 per cent of women in custody go on to receive a custodial sentence. They are generally on remand for 28 days: long enough to lose both home and children, with little chance of getting either back. They lose their tenancies, and the children are often taken into care. Indeed, 95 per cent of the children of women in prison have to leave the family home. On release, the local authority will not house them because they do not have children with them, and social services won't let them have their children because they have no suitable accommodation. This is where the downward spiral can begin.

And they self-harm, often to a truly shocking degree. Women make up less than 5 per cent of the prison population but are responsible for 51 per cent of self harm in the prison estate. That most of these women should not be in prison at all is obvious: what is required instead is diversion into the mental health system at an early stage, followed by support from women's centre projects, rather than community orders as these can be breached.

Finally – crucially – they have absolutely no life skills, often because they were brought up in such a way that they never learned any. Holding a conversation, working as part of a team, making a persuasive phone call, making and keeping an appointment are all skills which we learn, if we are lucky. But they are a major challenge for these women.

When the previous Government asked me to conduct a review of the vulnerabilities of women offenders and those at risk of offending – *The Corston Report* published in March 2007 – it was clear to me that what they needed was a way of turning their lives around, so that they could be responsible adults and effective parents. In short, they needed self-respect and self-confidence, the wellsprings of successful adult life. Prison did not and, during the short time offenders spent there, could not address any of these issues.

But I discovered a small number of women's community centres, generally run by women, which showed a different approach that actually focused on women: instead of sending women off on an odyssey through Whitehall – from the housing department, to the Department for Work and Pensions, via health and mental health services, debt advice, social services and the job centre, (none of which they could navigate on their own) – these women's centres arranged and managed appointments while working with the women to develop their life skills. The results were truly amazing. Recidivism rates were miniscule in comparison with the generally revolving door of women's repeat offending. They learned new skills and began to feel like citizens rather than pariahs. The economic case was overwhelming: I was told by Home Office officials that the total cost of imprisoning a woman for a year was £70,000. At the time, a place at the Asha Centre in Worcester cost £750. I know which is the better value for money.

In some parts of the country, like Halifax and Worcester, but also in Glasgow, the police and the courts recognised that these centres could play a crucial role in the rehabilitation of these women, and attendance at a centre gradually became an alternative sentence.

Much has happened in the succeeding four years since the report, with the Labour Government accepting most of my recommendations and starting the slow process of developing a network of centres around the country. They have been given financial assistance and expertise from the Corston Independent Funders' Coalition, comprising 21 charitable organisations coming together to support organisationas that divert women from custody. The present Government is continuing with this agenda. There are now over 40 projects nationwide, recently combined into a real network, supported by a central organisation, Women's Breakout. Some are probation focused, others have an open door policy, where statutory organisations and individuals can refer; in some, women can and do self-refer.

There are also a number of successful court advocacy schemes for women. In the Greater Bristol area, a female support worker attends court whenever a woman is due to appear before the bench, to assess her needs and situation. I heard of a woman charged with not paying her TV licence: a familiar route to prison for poor mothers. She had kept the TV on because her children wanted to be able to talk to their peers about current programmes. When she received the summons letter, she just ticked the 'guilty' box, which leads automatically to a fine of £1,500, and if she couldn't pay a £150 licence, the outcome is obvious. The support worker agreed to assist with debt repayment and benefit issues and the woman agreed to attend at a women's centre. A positive outcome all round.

As an illustration of how women can be either diverted from offending, or kept out of prison, the experience of the first year of the ISIS women's centre in Gloucester gives a very common picture. There were 364 referrals to the centre in its first year, to March 2011, 60 per cent having had involvement with the criminal justice system, most commonly serving a community order or on release from prison. The rest attended via statutory and voluntary sector agencies, as well as self-referral. Of these, 149 received crisis assistance or pre-assessment support. A total of 210 women went on to complete comprehensive assessments across the nine criminal justice resettlement 'pathways', and 194 had support plans put in place with regular key working arrangements to both support them and address their planned needs. Across nine different pathways (accommodation; skills, training and employment; health; drugs and alcohol; finance, debt and benefits; children, families and relationships; attitudes, thinking and behaviour; domestic violence, rape and abuse; and supporting women involved in prostitution) the outcomes were very impressive.

Of the women who came to the centre through the justice system, just 1 per cent had increased their offending.

As to the women who came to the centre through the criminal justice system, just 1 per cent of them had increased their offending, 13 per cent had stayed the same and 86 per cent had improved.

A couple of years ago, I was listening to Weekend Woman's Hour on Radio 4 and was surprised to hear my name. It was a piece on the experience of two women who had been through this process. They had thought the initial assessment a "load of rubbish". They had been asked questions such as what they had wanted to achieve when they were young, what their children and families thought of them, whether they thought they could ever hold down a job and provide for their children. But they stuck with it. At the end of the interview, they were asked what had happened to those initial assessment forms. One said it was on her fridge; the other had put it on her bedroom wall. Their children were proud of them. For me, that says it all.

6. How Prison Can Work

Phil Wheatley CB

Former Director General of the Prison Service Phil Wheatley argues that for prisons to improve, the whole system requires more stability and a clearer direction. If prisons are to be more than simply warehouses for prisoners, and the public better protected, some long-term and fundamental changes are required.

Imprisonment is the most severe punishment available to the courts; it is also the most expensive. Each year that someone spends in prison costs the taxpayer around £40,000. Though imprisonment is often regarded by tabloid newspapers as the only 'real' punishment, its high cost requires that careful and well-thought-through political decisions be taken about the extent of its use and how it is targeted.

Forty years in the Prison Service – including as Director General – tells me that we need a different approach to prisons. What is needed is a stable prison policy backed by adequate resourcing and sufficient prison places, with political decisions based on the evidence of what works.

This new approach is not more expensive than current ways of working with offenders. It needs to build on best practice but with a much more consistent and systemic approach to using existing front line staff time more productively. We need less emphasis on expensive professional input and seek to use mainstream community funding more productively by target-ing some on offenders. It does however require continued lev-els of resourcing that go beyond simply warehousing prison-ers, a practice that in any case is risky. Imprisonment without hope of improvement is inherently inhumane and will result in increased disorder and suicide.

These are all political choices. And they are expressed most strongly in the legislation laying down the sentencing options available to the courts. But this is not the only way that Ministers and other politicians can exert influence on sentencing; Ministers frequently set out their views on this issue in speeches, media briefing and interviews. These are often expressed forcefully and are sometimes openly critical of particular sentencing decisions. Without doubt this means that politicians do exert an influence on the judiciary, despite its avowed independence.

In contrast, without enacting primary legislation, Governments can vary the period of the prison sentence actually served. This is a device often used to quickly reduce the size of the prison population, when legislation and polit-ical messaging have produced higher numbers in custody than the Government can afford to resource. However, such short-term decisions risk undermining the public's faith that the sentence of the court actually means what it says.

This matters because prison plays a key role in helping to ensure that we have a stable and safe country. Rational use of imprisonment can only happen if there is clarity about the role it is intended to perform, and what it can realistically achieve. To ensure that public safety is maximised, we must also be clear about how integration will be achieved between prison and other key external services.

Those who work inside the system know that prison must be seen both by the public and by offenders as an effective punishment which is capable of acting to both deter crime and to reinforce a wider public faith in the system of law and order. In this context it is not sufficient to claim that deprivation of liberty is the only punishment. If this were true then simply putting a secure fence round a five star hotel would create an acceptable prison. Imprisonment must also constrain the lifestyle of prisoners so that the public see prison sentences as effective. This mean that prisoners can expect to be deprived of possessions like game consoles and computers and that privileges like conjugal visits should continue to be denied. This concept of relative deprivation changes over time and needs to be kept under review to ensure it takes account of changes in living standards in the wider community.

It is, however, also essential that in a just society punishment must be balanced with humanity. For imprisonment to be humane its pains must be bearable; it must feel just and fair to those undergoing it and must offer opportunities for personal improvement. Gratuitous cruelty, uncaring treatment of those in distress, denial of human rights or a failure to keep prisoners safe, healthy or to maintain their wellbeing are indefensible in a modern western democracy.

This matters not only because it is the only morally justifiable way of using imprisonment, but also because it is essential if prison is to be effective in reducing reoffending. Abusive imprisonment breeds resentment and hatred, reinforcing the view that offenders are in battle against society. This inevitably reinforces attitudes that make repeat crime more likely.

As a result of developments in modern criminology more is now understood about what gets offenders out of crime. It is worth recognising that in a basically deterrent-focused criminal justice system, those who are not deterred but continue to offend, will disproportionally include those who have little stake in society. This alienation from the mainstream may be because of poverty, experience of physical or emotional abuse, or may be the result of drug, alcohol and mental health problems. Very few of life's success stories appear in our criminal courts. This does not invalidate a deterrent system that demonstrably reinforces the non-criminal attitudes and behaviour of most citizens. It does mean for those who work to help offenders to give up crime that their work is difficult and has to take account of the social realities of the offenders they work with.

For repeat offenders who make up the bulk of the prison population, getting out of crime is difficult. It has something in common with the challenges many otherwise well-balanced people experience when trying to give up ingrained habits of behaviour like smoking, overeating or adultery.

For many offenders, crime has become a way of life and a solution to, or at least an escape from, their numerous problems. This will remain the case unless the offender can be motivated to want to change and can begin to visualize himself or herself as a no longer a criminal, and now able to lead a successful crime free life.

Key to getting the first step towards this change is for all the staff working directly with prisoners to have a genuine interest in offenders. They need to have insight and empathy, at the same time as having a realistic appreciation of the offender's criminality; they must be prepared to set boundaries and use their authority to enforce those boundaries.

Prison staff of different grades and from different professional backgrounds must work as a team, sharing information and ensuring that everything they do is fair and decent. In the context of a prison fairness and decency includes running a predictable regime that offers a variety of activity, with predictable and reasonable decisions and a willingness to listen to and explain decisions to prisoners. The prison must be kept safe and secure, and crime and indiscipline by those in custody must be dealt with firmly and fairly.

Once motivation is secured, the task is to build on it, reinforcing the new non-criminal identity by recognition, praise and opportunities to demonstrate it. Schemes inside prison that enable prisoners to help each other, to give help to their own families or to disadvantaged groups outside prison will strengthen the process of change. Giving them opportunities to develop skills through education and training, as well as through treatment to overcome drugs, alcohol, and mental health problems can also reinforce positive change.

Prisons are not Doctor Who's Tardis; their capacity is limited and places can only be used once.

Prisons also need an outward focus. Success will require preparation for the reality of release, so bringing outsiders in, including supportive friends or family members, is helpful particularly if they are able to continue this support outside prison. Getting prisoners engaged with activities that will support a non-criminal identity on release is also helpful; links to churches, mosques, and sports clubs are all good examples. Realistic plans also need to be made to gain housing and employment or training opportunities that will sustain the commitment to keep clear of crime.

This work inside must dovetail seamlessly for those released under licence with the supervision provided by the probation service. This implies free exchange of information before release, joint planning for release and a willingness for probation staff to work with offenders in a similar way.

When someone is really intent on giving up crime, success will also be aided if other key external agencies are willing to work with offenders to reinforce and build on what has been done in prison. Good intentions can be fatally weakened if for example, the only housing offered is alongside active criminals and drug users, or if mental health support is not continued outside for an offender stabilised in custody.

The public needs to be reassured that the sentence of the court will be served. Inflation in sentencing is as foolish as inflation in currency. The trade-offs in how prison places are used, in particular the balance between long, medium and short sentences needs to be grasped. Prisons are not Doctor Who's Tardis; their capacity is limited and places can only be used once. If too many places are occupied by long-term prisoners this leaves less capacity for shorter sentences. The shortest sentences offer few opportunities to engage with prisoners to reduce reoffending.

The prize to be pursued is the best use of taxpayers' money, a better-protected public, and a greater proportion of victims who see that the harm they suffered has helped to prevent more victims. It is not a panacea; there will still be failures, but fewer of them and we will need to continue to work with those failures so that next time they succeed.

Paul McDowell

Paul McDowell argues that breaking free from crime is more than about gaining basic skills and that the best way to do this, for non-violent offenders, can often be in the local community. Reading, writing, and arithmetic are crucial if offenders are to be rehabilitated and live a crime-free life outside prison.

Having spent 20 years working in the prison service before joining Nacro, I'm ashamed to admit it no longer shocks me that two-thirds of today's prison population have literacy levels below that of the average 11 year old and that the overwhelming majority of prisoners continue to face a plethora of barriers to employment upon release.

Many of the people I have worked with seem to struggle to solve life's day-to-day problems in a way which doesn't involve resorting to crime. Keeping appointments, using the telephone, handling money, finding somewhere to live, resolving interpersonal conflict and handling disputes all present major challenges for many offenders who have never learnt basic problem-solving skills. Their approach typically is a random one, the mental equivalent of tossing a coin to determine how they tackle problems. Inevitably and all too often, the approach involves criminal behaviour, taking them on an all-too-familiar return journey which ends, once more, behind bars.

Successive governments have grappled with the problem of what Sadiq Khan describes as the 'four Rs': reading, writing, arithmetic and rehabilitation. I have yet to meet a prison governor, past or present, who would argue against a more educative prison system. However, they would also argue that finding the solution is not straightforward. It is complex and difficult. They would point to a backdrop of record levels of incarceration, and a highly dysfunctional prison estate peppered with ageing establishments which are hardly conducive to acting as centres of learning. For many prisoners to break free from crime, it's not simply about addressing a basic skills deficit. They also need to tackle a multitude of other problems in their lives. What they need is a motivational approach to help them deal with these problems – an approach which isn't placed in jeopardy by constant moves around the prison estate, which maximises compliance, is joined up 'through the gate' back into our communities and which minimises attrition upon release. We must recognise that the place to teach people how to deal with life's realities is not inside a prison – which by definition is divorced from most people's reality – and the time to do it is not when the prisoner reaches adulthood, by which point an antisocial or criminal way of life may already be engrained.

The pressure currently placed on the prison system is significant. It faces ever-increasing demands to house more and more prisoners whilst handling significant cuts in resources. In the last two decades during the time I worked inside our prison system, prison numbers doubled to over 80,000. While this staggering increase in the use of imprisonment may well chime with the public's perceived appetite for punishment and general deterrence, it does not sit comfortably with the need to reduce crime – an overcrowded prison is not the most effective environment in which to educate offenders, deal with any associated alcohol, drug or mental illness problems, get them working, equip them for life on the outside and stop them offending when they come out.

The prison system is simply not geared up to addressing tens of thousands of prisoners' basic skills deficits and I question the viability of transforming the system as it is currently organised and configured, especially in a time of austerity. As Nacro's talented and experienced practitioners know, it takes time, patience and expertise to teach basic skills to offenders. It has to take place in consistent and focused learning environments in which learners feel safe and confident about learning. This is all very far removed from the rigid, one-size-fits-all approach currently applied in our prisons. It takes months, if not years, of collaborative learning, supported by mentors, coaches and tutors who understand offenders' frustrations, goals and limitations and who can help them overcome resistance and build their confidence to succeed, despite the fact they are very likely to have dropped out of, or been excluded from, school in childhood or adolescence. No matter how many advances have been made in the prison education system in recent years, a prisoner is seldom in one place long enough to benefit from the sort of positive learning environment so painstakingly built by my Nacro colleagues.

There is only one way I know of to make the prison system more educative: that is to create space for learning within it. Short of embarking on a massive (and unaffordable) prison building programme, the only sensible method of achieving this is to reduce the prison population, reserving it, incrementally, for those offenders who present the most serious risk to society. At a time when everyone wants to reduce reoffending, we must shift the focus of the debate from 'how do we make a punitive system more rehabilitative?' to 'how do we make a rehabilitative system sufficiently punitive to retain the confidence of the courts and the public at large?' And this shift in emphasis means that future providers of community sentences need to demonstrate improved reoffending outcomes on the one hand and better community confidence and involvement on the other.

Without doubt, public safety has to be the paramount concern. In seeking to scale down the prison population, the public must be presented with alternatives which are credible, effective and which reduce crime; over time this will increase public confidence. Robust non-custodial sentences would also make it eminently possible to improve offenders' reading, writing and problem-solving skills in the very communities where they encounter life's problems and in environments more conducive to learning than is ever likely to be possible within a prison. At the same time, this would create the headroom and the resources to improve educational facilities for those prisoners who do need to remain within our prisons.

This goes to the heart of why my colleagues at Nacro are calling for a policy push to transform community sentences. This call is in the pragmatic realisation, borne out of the experience of dealing with thousands of offenders in hundreds of communities, that in order to tackle reoffending and enable ex-offenders to make a positive contribution to their community, it is imperative to give them problem-solving skills and make them more job ready. We know this is made much more difficult to achieve if people who do not need to be sent to prison on public safety grounds are sent there anyway. We are less confident that community sentences, as currently configured and operated, offer a substantially better alternative. It remains the case that too many offenders fail to start their community orders, too many drop out after they have started, too few complete them, and too many go on to reoffend.

We therefore require a set of policies based on the notion of community justice. This involves the delivery of sentences which are demonstrably meaningful and relevant to the communities in which they are administered, as well as to the offenders who are subjected to them. This, in turn, requires restricting the offender's freedom of movement in such a way that intensive rehabilitative and reparative programmes can be attended night or day. At the same time, it demands greater involvement from the voluntary sector, which is uniquely placed to motivate offenders to participate and ensure that they derive the maximum benefit from interventions. Above all, it would involve incentivising the design and delivery of programmes which can deliver the right reductions in reoffending with large volumes of offenders over wide geographical areas.

We must avoid the temptation of implementing populist policies borne out of electoral motivations.

While easing the burden on the prison estate and re-engineering community sentences are necessary components in achieving community justice, they are not, of themselves, sufficient. We must also halt the current trend of reducing investment in youth crime prevention and early intervention targeted at young people who are most at risk of getting involved in crime. Following the implementation of the Crime and Disorder Act 1998, the rise of youth crime prevention and early intervention programmes had a positive impact on levels of youth crime in many of the country's highest crime neighbourhoods. The reason that they were effective was because they targeted those young people who were most at risk of offending. Using cross-sector partnerships embedded within local communities, the voluntary and community sector collaborated with parents, schools and youth offending teams to enable young people to minimise the impact of school exclusion and make the best of any other education opportunities, whether vocational or academic, so they could move their lives on and realise their true potential.

If we are to bring about change, it will require strong and determined leadership. We must avoid the temptation of implementing populist policies borne out of electoral motivations. Tackling offenders' basic skills deficits, although obvious and necessary, does not provide a panacea for reducing reoffending. In any event, educating offenders is not easily achieved within the prison setting nor, for that matter, with the current configuration of community sentences. For the education of prisoners to be successful, it must be tackled alongside the gamut of other problems facing the criminal justice system including the rise of the prison population, the inadequacies of community penalties and declining investment in local targeted prevention activities.

We need a ten-year community justice strategy which strikes an appropriate balance between punishment, attrition prevention, community involvement and public protection. The desired outcome for all of us is reductions all round: a reduction in crime, a reduction in the number of victims, a reduction in the levels of fear of crime in communities and, hardest of all, a reduction in reoffending.

8. Eyes Wide Shut

Lord Victor Adebowale

It is no easy task to provide solutions for substance misuse and mental health problems and it is unrealistic to expect their complete eradication, says Victor Adebowale. We need to ensure that services in prisons provide an effective response that supports the individual to address their problems.

Up until the day he died, I'd have to say that Jim was basically a good, intelligent and gentle guy. A couple of misguided smack injections have a very ugly habit of turning honest taxpaying citizens into drug-craving thieves though. When someone commits a crime, it is important that there are consequences for that person, be it in terms of serving time or 'fessing up to who they are and what they've done. Sometimes it's essential to take people off the streets who are a danger to the communities they terrorise. Other times we take people off the streets, bang them up, and turn them out again into far more devastating circumstances then we could have imagined.

In Jim's case he was put in prison for six months because he'd got into petty theft to fund his addiction. It was agony coming off the drugs – indeed, he did everything he could to stay on them while in prison. When I visited him, I remember him telling me how tennis balls and even dead pigeons came hurtling over the walls from the world outside. The stuffed illicit contents of these projectiles kept many of the prisoners going while they served their time, but for whatever reason, Jim was one of the few who couldn't get his hands on these imports. In the circumstances, and with the right guidance and help Jim actually managed to stay off drugs while he was in prison, and he eventually left custody clean and ready to resume the good times, when his life hadn't revolved around drugs and crime.

But I think you already know how this story ends, and as a society we should be ashamed that we didn't give Jim the support he needed once he'd got out of prison to maintain the ground he'd made. With the continuity of support, I'd bet you that Jim would be working hard, paying tax, and enjoying family life right now. But Jim came out of prison to find nothing. No one had guided him to the right service, let alone met him at the prison gates to ensure he got there. Four months later he took what used to be a normal heroin dose to him, but his drug-free body couldn't handle it any more and he died.

Today, there is still no easy way to provide solutions for substance misuse and mental health problems within prison, and we certainly cannot expect to see their complete eradication. What we really need to ensure is that services in prisons can provide an effective response that supports the individual so they can face their problems and step outside of the spiralling circumstances that inevitably lead to being banged up again and again and again.

The challenge for the prison system is how we make sure that prisons – by their nature large institutions – are able to respond to individual prisoners. Prisons have multiple functions: at once we expect them to punish and deter and also to rehabilitate so that offenders can leave the criminal justice system altogether. All these functions are designed to reduce crime, yet the statistics show prison has not been particularly effective in achieving this. It is difficult to find any sense of pride in the fact that 59 per cent of offenders who receive a prison sentence of less than a year are reconvicted within 12 months of release.[1]

When we look at these statistics we must not forget that the criminal justice system has contact with some of the most vulnerable people in society. Believe it or not, a lot of them are not bad people. More often than not, they are people who are enduring complex needs, which should have been addressed in the health and social care system before crime was even able to rear its head. But even in prison – the last bastion for a late intervention – these people are not getting effective support, and their complex needs are left unaddressed.

By way of illustration, the following statistics form the tip of the iceberg:

- Over half of prisoners report their offence was connected to their substance misuse.[2]
- Eight in ten male remand prisoners who are drug dependent had two additional mental disorders.[3]
- Of the more than 80,000 prisoners in England and Wales it is estimated that nine out of ten have one or more mental health disorders.[4]
- There can be up to 39,000 drug users in the prison system at any one time.[5]

Of course, individuals must accept responsibility for their actions, but prisons must also provide the opportunity for offenders to do this. The bottom line is that prisons have not been an effective environment to help individuals challenge their mental health and substance misuse problems. For instance, almost a fifth of those respondents who had ever used heroin say they first started using the drug whilst in custody.[6]

This worrying figure demonstrates that within the pressure cooker of prison, people's needs can become more amplified, further impeding their rehabilitation.

To improve mental health and substance misuse services within prisons, you've got to appreciate that these conditions are very often related to a number of interlinked and mutually reinforcing social factors. It is not possible to treat the complexities of substance misuse and mental health in isolation: the person and their own individual perceptions of their problems must be central in any attempts to support them.

At the heart of this is what we call 'integrated care'. This is not limited to just integration of services within prison, although this is of vital importance; it is also about integration with services within the community to ensure continuity of service provision when an offender is released. The need for this approach can be seen in research which suggests that 96 per cent of prisoners with a mental health difficulty returned to their communities without any supported housing – and more than three quarters of them had no follow-up appointment with community support services whatsoever.[7] If someone who has been addressing a health problem while on the inside isn't given the stability they need to maintain their gains on the outside, then we all know what consequences are likely. For Jim, they were just plain lethal.

Progress made by individuals while they are in prison to address their mental health problems and substance misuse is likely to be very fragile. The dislocation between support received in prison and follow-on support in the community can only make progress that much harder. People often fall through the cracks when they are released from prison and they do not access the support they need. I've heard the disgraced former Tory MP, Jonathan Aitken, describe his first-hand experience of this when he was sentenced to do time in HMP Belmarsh. It was there, and later as an onlooker at HMP Brixton, that he saw drug dealers lingering around the prison gates because they know this is the best place to pick up new clients. If health or social professional aren't there to meet ex-offenders at the gate, all too often it'll be the dealers who meet them – right when they're at their most vulnerable.

The prison population has very specific characteristics which make the integration of services challenging. In 2010 the Patel Report, commissioned by the Department of Health, astutely highlighted the difficulties of achieving continuity of care within prisons when an offender can be transferred up to four times over the course of a single sentence.[8] Similarly, once they are released, offenders can very often move around the country, creating difficulties for the maintenance of support.

The prison population has very specific characteristics which make the integration of services challenging.

Nowhere is integration more necessary than in the treatment of dual diagnosis (the co-existence of both substance misuse and mental health difficulties). It is estimated that 26 per cent of the prison population have a dual diagnosis. However, the prison inspectorate found no signs of consistent dual diagnosis provision.[9] It is important that a multi-disciplinary approach is taken to respond to dual diagnosis and a care plan for an offender should be co-ordinated across all teams involved in their support. In particular, this will prevent one diagnosis being given prominence over another. For example, I've seen plenty of people getting treatment for a drug addiction, but very little attention to the underlying reason why they were taking drugs in the first place – depression. You have to look at all aspects together.

Similarly, substance misuse services within prisons have often failed to acknowledge the negative effects of alcohol – focusing mainly on drugs instead. The Inspectorate of Prisons has identified that at every stage of prison the needs of offenders who misuse alcohol are less likely to be addressed than those who misuse illicit drugs.[10] Granted, it's a lot trickier to stuff a can of Super into a pigeon, but the story for the prisoner is the same. They don't drink while they're in prison. But when they get out, what's the first thing they do? Get smashed. And what do they do the next day? Get smashed. And then a while later, they're smashed again, only this time they've just put someone in a coma when things got out of hand. That the holistic needs of the individual have not been met is further demonstrated by the fact that CARATs (Counselling, Assessment, Referral Advice and Throughcare services) have previously not been funded to work with offenders experiencing alcohol problems. At least with drugs, you can get treatment.

Nevertheless, there are some positive signs that the deficiencies of substance misuse and mental health services within prisons have been recognised. There has been the acknowledgement of the need for integration within the coalition Government's reforms to public services. For instance, substance misuse treatment both in prison and the community is being brought into the public health remit. There are even plans to introduce drugs recovery wings within several prisons which will accept offenders with short sentences who are experiencing substance misuse difficulties. I'd like to optimistically think that with the help of decent Third Sector organisations like Turning Point, these drug-free wings might even address someone's alcohol use too. This is certainly something we're looking at achieving under the Government's emerging Payment by Results prison pilots.

Support has also been expressed by the Government for the findings of the 2009 Bradley Report. The Government is beginning to put in place many of the Review's 81 recommendations for specialist approaches to helping people with mental health and learning disability issues address their difficulties and significantly reduce reoffending. The Health and Criminal Justice Board, who are charged with overseeing the implementation of these recommendations, has an important role to play in ensuring the recommendations of the Review are not lost, and it is important that this Board doesn't fall foul of the current cuts to public services.

Above all, what we really need are effective services. And effective services can only be created through effective commissioning processes. The previous increase in the level of drug treatment in prisons, although welcome, was met with increasing complexity through the creation of multiple funding streams and commissioning routes. The latest commissioning guidance for substance misuse services in prison acknowledges the need to link with offender health commissioning, as well as stating there will be one funding pot for both prison and community services. Despite these promising signs, there are still unanswered questions about the reforms to the commissioning process for both mental health and substance misuse services, not least in terms of what happens during those vital minutes and hours after someone walks through the prison gate.

What is more, the split between local commissioning processes for community services and the work of the NHS Commissioning Board has the potential to fragment mental health care for offenders with severe conditions. There is a great deal of discussion around integration within the reforms to the NHS, and it is vital these discussions turn into reality and all parts of the health system function well together. While Health and Wellbeing Boards will be important to achieve this, responsibility for pursuing integration should be shared and owned across the health, social care and public health spheres to ensure a sense of joint accountability. At least then there will be people who will have to answer when the likes of Jim meet their unfortunate death. When Jim died, the state had done so conveniently little, that no one needed to answer for his death.

But with reform there is hope, and the reforms to commissioning are intended to make services much more responsive to the needs of individuals. It is important the interactions across different agencies which have contact with the offender are fully co-ordinated and it cannot be underestimated how the actions of one agency impacts another.

But how can we learn if we're not listening to the people in receipt of these services? Although there has been progress in working to rectify the deficiencies of mental health and substance misuse prison services, little has been said about ensuring the voice of the offender is central to the structure and commissioning of services. It is of little use to streamline the commissioning process if insufficient attention is paid to understanding offenders' needs and their perception of how services can be made better.

While the recent debates on the reform of the criminal justice system have been positive in their focus on rehabilitation, I have yet to see evidence of how we will systematically ensure we understand the weaknesses of current service provision from the offender's point of view. This may prove politically difficult but I would point out that concern about money being wasted on ineffective services is far more contentious to the electorate.

While we can always expect to see people with mental health and substance misuse problems within prisons, I think there is a lot that can be done to improve services. Offenders are individuals and we should not assume they all have the same problems. Yes, they should be punished for the crimes they've committed, but as we undergo this Rehabilitation Revolution, isn't it even more important that we seize the opportunity to get the rehab bit right too? Therefore, services need to have the flexibility to respond to individual need. This requires a multi-disciplinary approach focusing on robust care co-ordination and allowing adequate opportunities for the identification of problems.

The criminal justice system is a complex web of different organisations, all with their own remit and approach. However, these agencies must interact better together – along with community services in the prisoner's home area – to maintain stability and continuity of care. Without this, any progress made while the offender has been in prison is likely to be lost, and it is society that will pay the price. Usually we pay when the *ex*-offender becomes the *re*-offender, but sometimes we pay when someone as promising as Jim dies before our wide open (or should I say wide *shut*) eyes.

Footnotes

1 Ministry of Justice (2011), Adult Re-convictions: Results from the 2009 Cohort, London: Ministry of Justice
2 Ramsay, M. (ed.) (2003) Prisoners' drug use and treatment: seven studies, Home Office Research Findings 186, London: Home Office
3 Office of National Statistics
4 Policy Exchange (2008) Out of Sight, Out of Mind: The state of mental healthcare in prison
5 HM Prison Service Drug Strategy Unit (2003). Prison Service Drug Strategy.
6 Ministry of Justice (2010) Compendium of reoffending statistics and analysis, London: Ministry of Justice.
7 Edgar, K., and Rickford, D. (2009) Too little too late: an independent review of unmet mental health need in prison, London: Prison Reform Trust
8 Prison Drug Treatment Strategy Review (2010) Reducing Drug-Related Crime and Rehabilitating Offenders

9   The Offender Health Research Network (2009), A National Evaluation of Prison Mental Health In-Reach Services, Manchester: University of Manchester and HM Chief Inspector of Prisons for England and Wales (2010) Annual Report 2008-09, London: HM Inspectorate of Prisons

10 HM Chief Inspector of Prisons for England and Wales (2010) Alcohol services in prisons: an unmet need, London: HMCIP

References

Edgar, K. and Rickford, D., *Too Little, Too Late: An Independent Review of Unmet Mental Health Need in Prison*, 2009, Prison Reform Trust

HM Chief Inspector of Prisons for England and Wales (2010), *Alcohol services in prisons: an unmet need*, London: HMCIP

HM Chief Inspector of Prisons for England and Wales (2010) Annual Report 2008-09, London: HM Inspectorate of Prisons

HM Prison Service Drug Strategy Unit (2003). Prison Service Drug Strategy. London: HM Prison Service

Ministry of Justice (2011), *Adult Re-convictions: Results from the 2009 Cohort*, London: Ministry of Justice

Ministry of Justice (2010) *Compendium of reoffending statistics and analysis*, London: Ministry of Justice.

Out of Sight, Out of Mind: The state of mental healthcare in prison (2008) By Professor Charlie Brooker & Ben Ullmann. London: Policy Exchange

Prison Drug Treatment Strategy Review (2010) Reducing Drug-Related Crime and Rehabilitating Offenders

Ramsay, M. (ed.) (2003) Prisoners' drug use and treatment: seven studies, Home Office Research Findings 186, London: Home Office

The Offender Health Research Network (2009), A National Evaluation of Prison Mental Health In-Reach Services, Manchester: University of Manchester

9. Ready for the Real World of Work

Kevin McGrath

Only a quarter of prisoners have a job to go to on their release and this is a big cause of reoffending, argues Kevin McGrath. Rather than just focusing on qualifications, prisoners should do real work in prison as part of their rehabilitation. Working for local employers to meet skills deficits will also demonstrate work – rather than crime – pays.

It's time to abandon the soft option on prisons. If the continuous wave of repeat offences by former inmates is to be tackled seriously, some courageous political and judicial changes will be necessary.

The soft option has been in place since prisons were first created and it still operates across the prison estate today: it is the one based on a tenet of locking 'em up until they've done their time. It's a soft option because it is driven by, and appeals to, a simplistic public and media clamour for punishment which outweighs – not least when it comes to politicians' responses – the more complex arguments for paths to rehabilitation. There are numerous rehabilitation programmes which offer exceptions to the rule, some of which are highly successful, but they are piece-meal, nationally unco-ordinated, underfunded and, in terms of the big picture, ineffective. Ineffective in preventing crime through reoffending and ineffective in terms of best value for taxpayers' money. A prison regime which simply turns 50 to 70 per cent of offenders out to offend again is a self-defeating waste of money and purpose. And it fails the offenders themselves.

The alternative option is harder because it will attract the wrath of the vocal 'bang 'em up and throw away the key' brigade – from the *Daily Mail* to the right wing of the Conservative party, will require sophisticated thinking and joined-up action and, perhaps above all if it is to work, the unfaltering strength of conviction from politicians, policy makers and prison authorities. The message is that to reduce rates of re-offending, inmates need jobs, a home, a bank account and ideally a stable family life on their release. To get jobs they need education and real work experience while they in prison. If offenders are working, re-offending rates are reduced, there is less crime, there are fewer victims, and the offender starts to contribute to society by paying tax. All of which means a better life for them and us all.

Yet, according to the annual report of the National Offender Management Service, only 26 per cent of prisoners had jobs following their release last year. Every day a prisoner will be released with no job into the catch-22 of re-offending. Without a job they cannot get a home and vice versa. Without a job they cannot open a bank account. The path back to further crime usually takes no longer than two weeks for those who re-offend.

That there is an alternative is exemplified by a project run within High Down prison in Surrey called The Clink, a high class prison restaurant operated by inmates and open to the public. The catering courses allow inmates to qualify up to Level Four on the NCQ and City and Guilds scale, which gives them a better chance of a job on the outside. Most other educational courses in prison offer a maximum Level Two grade which is not as convincing to prospective employers. More than 25 offenders have left the course and the prison for jobs and the level of offending rate is low, at 20 per cent. The key to The Clink's success is that it offers a genuine working environment, with tangible results and job satisfaction with real customers to satisfy. It is not designed merely to occupy the time of prisoners but to generate genuine, interested engagement, a motivation to break the vicious circle and hope, through credible evidence of results, that there might be a job to go to and a crime-free future outside. These elements are crucial to any comprehensive plan to reduce re-offending through training.

The average prisoner is likely to have had poor experiences of education and employment: almost half of male prisoners have been excluded from school and two thirds have a reading ability below that of an 11 year old. Two thirds of those entering prison are unemployed. However, prisoners are also likely to have skills which would help them succeed in business, ingenuity, salesmanship and risk–taking for a start.

But innate skills must be nurtured towards a tangible outcome, rather than just a qualification for qualifications' sake. Mainstream education has evolved from deskbound teaching to practical application; primary school teachers regularly take lessons out of the classroom to help children of all abilities conceptualise their work. Apprenticeships have been hailed as the 'gold standard' because they combine learning and training, yet offender learning is, as ever, lagging behind.

The current prison industries system aims to "occupy prisoners in out-of-cell activity and wherever possible to help them gain skills, qualifications and work experience". While a 2003 review found that "industrial workshops are one of the best means, within prison walls, to reflect real working life" there are currently only 10,000 workshop places available (only 11 per cent of the currently prison population) providing largely unskilled work with little opportunity to train or develop.

Whereas, traditionally, prison industry only provided for the internal market, the Ministry of Justice (MoJ) is increasingly contracting with business to provide basic manufacturing and services. However, even with business involvement, this system is far removed from 'real working life'. Prisoner time is a commodity which the MoJ sells – there is no relationship between the business and the worker, and wages are set at a token rate by the prison. The regime does not support working hours and the average prisoner spends only 24 hours in purposeful activity each week. In addition, we are already seeing purposeful activity decrease as specifically trained officers are redistributed to core security duty, a trend which is sure to continue as cuts kick in.

The Howard League for Penal Reform has long promoted the concept of real work in prison and numerous reports have been published by government and think tanks into the practicality of operating working prisons. The Howard League's Barbed project began in 2005 and was the first time a business had operated within a prison, hiring prisoner employees and paying a fair wage. Employees were trained in graphic design and production and worked full time to build a business that was viable. However, the project highlighted institutional barriers that need to be overcome.

We need to demonstrate that work – and not crime – pays. We need to give people responsibility by creating mechanisms for paying tax, contributing to living costs, victim funds and enable them to save for their resettlement. Currently there is no system to allow prisoners to pay tax, so even if a business decided to pay real wages, Her Majesty's Revenue and Customs (HMRC) would not process their employees' contribution.

The Howard League has made practical recommendations about how real work could function in a ring-fenced group of specialist prisons, with a taxation and contribution system which encourages participation from businesses and the prison service. A key consideration in the setting of remuneration is to promote a healthy market, not one that undercuts local businesses or exploits prison labour.

The Government has announced a 'rehabilitation revolution', incorporating competition from the voluntary and private sector to bring about a 10 per cent cost saving to the prisons and probation services. But, at the same time as 30,000 prisoners are entering the system each quarter, budget cuts, not rehabilitation, appear to be the overriding priority and the Government is increasingly reliant on external partners to provide services at the same time as cutting vital

Positive noises made by the Government are undermined by falling budgets and an unwillingness to reform structures.

funding. External organisations often feel they are fighting against the prison service, rather than working with it and this feeling will only be exacerbated as cuts are imposed inside and outside prison. Education staff feel isolated and removed from the running of the prison and governors have little knowledge or say about what takes place in education. Positive noises made by the Government are undermined by falling budgets and an unwillingness to re-evaluate and reform the prison and probation service structures (which offer no comprehensive rehabilitation programme and were never designed to cope with such high numbers going through the system). These are critical issues which Labour's own review must address.

A full working week, rather than the average 24 hours of purposeful activity which currently takes place; an education and training provision which is collaborative, rather than departments operating in silos; the opportunity to train and work for local employers meeting local skills deficits, rather than prisoners being housed far from home with little opportunity to connect with the community they'll return to; a real wage for real work, and a mechanism to make a positive financial contribution to society. These are all measures that, on a larger scale, would make training more meaningful in a rehabilitative sense.

However, it remains to be seen how effective these initiatives will be when, in between July and September 2011, there were only 462,000 vacancies and 2.62 million people out of work. Rehabilitation is not possible through retraining alone; it must be addressed holistically alongside wider criminal justice, education and welfare policy in the wider community.

10. Stopping Young Offenders Becoming Adult Offenders

Shauneen Lambe

Children who go to prison often spend their whole lives in and out of it. Shauneen Lambe speaks to 'F' – who managed to break the cycle of re-offending having been in trouble with the police from a young age – about how to help young people who have become involved in crime and how to stop them from getting involved in the first place.

I returned to the UK from Louisiana USA in 2003 where I had been representing children facing the death penalty. It was a relief to come back to the relative safety of the UK, where the state did not try to kill their children. However it was quickly apparent that poverty, here as in the US, is a catalyst for children entering the criminal justice system. I have been representing young people in court for many years and they are rarely middle class kids; if they are it is usually because they have a disability such as autism and their parents seek me out. Once children are in the criminal justice system, breaking the pattern becomes harder and harder. While there are no simple solutions, it is glaringly apparent that, as with health costs, prevention is cheaper than cure.

Aika Stephenson and I set up Just for Kids Law in 2006; Aika came to the work from the statutory sector of the Youth Offending Team, I as a lawyer. We both realised there was a desperate need for young people to receive wrap-around support. Representing them effectively in court or on orders is essential but only deals with the immediate problem. There are usually other systemic issues that lead a child into offending behaviour, be that a learning disability, being out of education (when we first undertook an analysis of our clients we discovered 85 per cent were out of mainstream education), unstable accommodation, lack of family support, irregular immigration status, exploitation. We provide tailored support to every young person we work with and we make a difference. It may not be immediate, although sometimes it is, but over time we notice the young people we work with become more engaged and always come back to us when they need assistance.

F is a great example. He is currently in his 2nd year at university studying Criminology and Law and to support his studies he works at Marks and Spencer. He trains lawyers and other professionals with Just for Kids Law. He is a Youth Ambassador for us and talks to journalists and policy makers about youth justice. Prior to his involvement with Just for Kids Law he was excluded from school and in trouble with the law.

F and our other young people tell us that all they want to do is to be able to support themselves, but that is so difficult to do. There is no one to help them get jobs, school seems to have no practical application and bureaucracy makes it difficult too. When presented with ways of making money that are illegal, people choose to go into that. What we need to do, as a society, is to give all kids equal opportunities to work and they will work hard.

Another difficulty for the young people we work with is that they are magnets for the police. There are not many places for young people to go, so they are out on the streets and are easy targets. We see the police outside our local schools at the end of the day; there are none outside the private schools. They are therefore more likely to be drawn into the criminal justice system by the police 'doing their jobs' and, once labelled, the spiral begins.

SL – *Who were you most influenced by – your friends or your family?*

F – Group mentality always overshadows your parents, I was always doing things to impress my friends, all of these friends are now in prison. Some young people also have pressure from families to provide money, most of the kids I know were having to provide money for their family. Families are unable to live off their income so there is an expectation for the kids to bring in more. I think there should be no fines for young people in court, of course they don't have the money, the people who get punished are my family, why should they be punished they haven't done anything wrong?

> *We see the police outside our local schools at the end of the day; there are none outside the private schools*

SL – *In 2008 the United Kingdom was criticised by the UN Committee on the Rights of the Child for the 'general climate of intolerance and negative public attitudes towards children, especially adolescents'. Did you feel you were labelled as you were growing up?*

F – I was always told I was naughty, I was easily distracted, after a while you begin to believe it. We are put down so much in our life from teachers, police officers, youth workers

– we are made to feel like shit. These people are always pointing the bad in you.

SL – *How do you think we can stop young people getting involved in crime or help them stop once they have got involved?*

F – I was different from my friends, I was lucky, I got help from Just for Kids Law. You helped me when I was out of school to get back into education and by working with you I was inspired into going to law school. You would involve me in events, I would see that patience would get you things in life. I thought to myself these people believe in me, I am training lawyers and they are listening to me, I can do something and people will listen.

The thing that really helps is someone seeing good in you, that is sometimes all it takes. Too many times kids are told how bad they are. But if someone believes in you it gives you hope that you can do something in your life. Praise gives people a bit of motivation. I think Just for Kids should try and help all kids who are getting in trouble.

Government can also reward young people, like EMA [Educational Maintenance Allowance] for being in education. It was only £30 but when you were studying hard you looked forward to having a treat at the end of the week.

People should be rewarded for doing things well as well as punished for doing things wrong.

SL – *Statistics show that in England and Wales we lock up more children than any other European country and re-offending rates amongst locked up young peoples are really high, nearly 72 per cent. Why do you think going to prison has such high rates of re-offending?*

F – Everyone knows prison doesn't work. I can't believe that powerful people think it works. When I was 16 I didn't mind going to prison, in fact I wanted to go to prison that was where all the G's (Gangsters) were at – the real criminals. They were the people I respected, the people in jail. I wanted to be like them, they were my idols. If you send young people there they will find their idols, if you keep them with positive people in the community they might make them their idols.

There needs to be positive role models around children, people that you can look up to who you want to grow up to be. When I started working with Just for Kids Law that was when I found my role models because you talked to me on my level, you helped young people out and you were respected by powerful people. That is what made me want to become a lawyer.

SL – *Statistics show that really well run, well-funded community and restorative projects are much more effective than prison, for example 'Youth Conferencing' in Northern Ireland. Do you agree?*

F – Rehabilitation does work, these people are still kids, they are still learning. If you have a little kid you have to teach them everything about right from wrong and they gradually learn that. We don't expect to tell a kid something one time and for them never to do it again, there has to be time where they mess up and we tell them again and then eventually they will learn. For example even when I was working with Just for Kids I messed up and you lot would look at me and tell me that you were disappointed but it was different from being told I was bad, it was like you could see the good in me but I wasn't making the most of my life, I felt like I had let you down and myself down.

In the UK we live in a multi-cultural society where there are different views as to what is acceptable behaviour and we need to give people time to adapt to the world in which they live in.

SL – *The European Court of Human Rights implies that the UK is not acting in the best interests of children by putting them through criminal proceedings. Do you think the best way to deal with children who are getting in trouble is through an adversarial court such as the youth court or the crown court?*

F – The first time I was arrested I was refused bail, I was kept in the police station all weekend – that mentally fucked my head. I spent the whole weekend just looking at that blue mattress, there was nothing to do for the whole weekend.[1]

When I was taken to court I didn't understand anything that went on. I was 16 at the time, I had only seen it on the media. I felt so much pressure being there, from the judge and the prosecution, my heart was pounding, my instinct was to get up and run, I actually thought about getting up and running and this was just the youth court. I didn't understand anything that was being said, I was relying on my lawyer, she reassured my family. All you want is your lawyer to do the best for you. Many lawyers are just doing it for the money, but in the end it is you that is going to prison not them.

If I had been in court at the age of 10, I think I would have lost it, I would have been physically and mentally fucked up, I would have got post traumatic stress disorder. A 10 year old is not allowed to decide to smoke cigarettes or drink alcohol yet we say they are able to decide and responsible enough to commit a crime? At the age of 10 I am still going through what is right or wrong, I am still in primary school. How terrifying is that? Seriously?

SL – *If you were a politician how would you change the court system for children and young people?*

F – I would have understood much better if things had been presented in a way a kid would understand it. It seemed like there were so many unnecessary people in the court, I didn't know who they were: the prosecution, the youth offending team, I felt like I was on trial for murder and this was only the youth court. If you think about sitting with a head teacher being told off, you are already scared, let alone being tried in front of a judge.

Footnotes

1 This procedure, although in breach of the Children Act is a common occurrence at police stations, Howard League statistics show that in 2008-2009 53,000 children were kept in police stations overnight 13,000 of these were aged between 9-13.

11. What Causes Crime?

Professor Robert Reiner

Being 'tough on crime and tough on the causes of crime' was always more than just a sound bite. Robert Reiner asks; what are the preconditions for a criminal act? And, when so many crimes – including those that go unrecognised by the legal system – go unpunished, how can we distinguish between crime and criminality?

The ultimate cause of most crime is social injustice and there is a mass of evidence to support this. Acknowledging this does not excuse those who commit crimes, but if we are serious about wanting to protect potential victims it is necessary to probe these deeper roots of bad behaviour. Offenders are usually responsible for the harm they do – but so are we responsible for seeking to tackle its ultimate causes in the increasingly unjust and amoral societies we live in.

What is crime?

"Sheer criminality" (Theresa May); "criminality pure and simple" (David Cameron). What can these reactions to this summer's riots possibly mean? Is 'criminality' used only as a synonym for 'criminal behaviour'? If so, why not just say 'crimes'?

Smuggled into their use of the (supposedly 'pure and simple') word 'criminality' there is a controversial conservative theory about the causation of crime: that crime is solely due to lack of control, and that therefore firmly reasserting discipline is the effective antidote. Condensed within this are a variety of debates about why control becomes inadequate. It is axiomatic that crime is behaviour *chosen* by offenders. Nonetheless there are factors making failure to exercise self-control more likely.

In conservative theories the usual suspects are either pathological characteristics of particular cultures (David Starkey's 'analysis' of black culture being a recent egregious example), or they describe the malign legacy of what they see as growing liberal dominance of the common culture, (as when Melanie Phillips laments 'permissiveness' and the 1960s). These claims are grossly limited by their blinkered focus on the single dimension of control. It is like explaining the speed and direction of a car solely in terms of the driver's skill with the brake.

The concepts of 'crime' and 'criminality' cannot be described as 'pure and simple'. The Oxford English Dictionary defines crime as "An act punishable by law, as being forbidden by statute or injurious to the public welfare … An evil or injurious act; an offence, sin; esp. of a grave character." Even this definition is far from 'pure and simple': many acts that are 'injurious to the public welfare' are not 'forbidden by statute' – for example tax avoidance, to take a currently critical illustration. As the subtitle of Nicholas Shaxson's recent book *Treasure Islands* indicates, the legal tax havens he analyses are devices by which wealthy people have 'stolen the world' in ways that are *not* forbidden by law. And the last set of definitions point to other notions of crime that are not necessarily legally prohibited – varying conceptions of grave sin, evil or injury.

All these definitions – legal, moral, social – are much wider-ranging than the problem of crime as constructed by the criminal justice system, let alone media and political debate. From the start (stop and search) to the end (imprisonment) of the criminal justice process the overwhelming focus is on economically and socially marginalised young men, disproportionately from minority ethnic backgrounds. As the American criminologist Jeffrey Reiman pithily sums it up in the title of his classic book, *The Rich Get Richer and the Poor Get Prison* (and, we should add, they get victimised by crime too).

It is a hotly debatable point whether this profile represents those who actually commit crimes or those who are unlucky enough to be caught. Since only around 2 per cent of crimes recorded by the British Crime Survey result in a conviction it is impossible to be confident that the characteristics of identified offenders correspond to the overall pattern of perpetrators. Almost certainly, the ranks of those who escape being identified as criminal consist disproportionately of the privileged and powerful. In practice the criminal justice system is not an apparatus for controlling crime in general, but only a small range of 'street' offences.

'Criminality' by contrast connotes a propensity to produce crime. Biological and psychological theories have postulated a variety of factors supposedly marking out some individuals as more likely to commit crimes: from body type to genetic predispositions, from low IQ to maternal deprivation. Social theories analyse criminality as the propensity of societies to generate higher or lower levels of crime. The understanding of crime, whether at the macro level of broad trends or patterns, or the micro level of specific incidents, involves a weaving together of different elements and levels of explanation. It also requires recognition both of the choices and responsibility of perpetrators, *and* how these are framed and influenced by social processes implicating our political economy and culture more broadly.

Crime's complex preconditions

For a crime to occur there are several logically necessary preconditions: labelling, motive, means, opportunity, and the absence of control.

Labelling

Apparent shifts in crime rates and patterns may frequently be due to labelling processes. Changes in criminal law or criminal justice procedures, and in patterns of reporting and recording incidents, can have major influences on apparent patterns and trends in crime. For example, major reforms in 1998 and 2002 of the rules governing police compilation of statistics undoubtedly expanded the range of incidents included, considerably increasing the recorded rate of crime. In the 1970s the spread of household contents insurance induced more victims to report offences, sparking an apparent surge of burglary.

Labelling may also act as a cause of criminal behaviour itself. Changes in how people treat identified offenders (stigmatisation, ostracism, denial of jobs) may contribute to further offending, as may alterations in a convicted person's self-identity. Whether the crime-producing consequences of official reactions to deviance outweigh their crime-control effects cannot be settled once and for all; it is an open empirical question in particular circumstances.

Motivation

Detective fiction and the newspapers tend to portray the motives driving crime as complex, puzzling, often bizarre, requiring the sensitivity of a Dostoevsky or a Freud – or at least an Agatha Christie or a Cracker – to unravel. This is because they tend to focus on extremely unusual, very serious, pathologically violent and sexual cases. In real life, most offences are committed for quite conventional and readily comprehensible reasons, prompted by motives that are widely shared – money, fashionable goods, sexual pleasure, excitement, thrills, and intoxication by alcohol, adrenalin or other drugs. Offenders are not driven by deviant values but rather by their conventional immersion in the values and desires of a contemporary consumer culture which simultaneously denies them legitimate means of attainment.

Cultures that emphasise material and monetary success generate strains towards deviance at all levels of society, not least amongst elites.

The fact that most crime is motivated by mundane, widely shared aspirations and pursuits does not, however, mean that understanding motives is unimportant in unravelling crime trends. Social, cultural and economic changes affect the pressures and attractions of behaviour labelled as criminal, increasing or decreasing the numbers of people motivated to commit them.

The seminal account of how macro-social structures can affect variations in motivations to commit crime between cultures and over time is Robert Merton's classic theory of *anomie*, first developed in the 1930s to explain why the USA was the Western world's crime capital. Structurally-limited legitimate opportunities generate pressures for crime, not automatically, but in cultures that encourage widespread aspirations for everyone through a mythological fable of the possibility of rising from rags to riches – epitomised by the 'American Dream'. Cultures that emphasise material and monetary success generate strains towards deviance at *all* levels of society, not least – indeed perhaps above all – amongst elites. There is no terminal point for monetary aspirations, and success breeds desire rather than satisfaction. Winning is all that counts. Conceptions of proper and legitimate means get pushed aside: nice guys or gals finish last; losers are zeroes. Cutting corners, coming first, is all that matters, at all levels of society and all times. Deviance becomes the new normal. The recent parliamentary expenses scandals, the revelations of the corrupt networks linking politicians, police and press, and – at the other end of the social scale – what have been called 'the shopping riots', are all testimony to the power of this 70-year-old theory.

Means of crime

As lovers of detective mysteries know, in addition to motive criminals need means and opportunity. The commission of crime requires a variety of personal and technical resources. Changes in political economy, culture, technology, and social patterns can expand or contract the *means* of committing crimes. New types of crime become possible, old ones are blocked off, and new ways of committing old offences are created. Innovative means of exchange, from cheques, then credit cards, and more recently the internet, have provided successive new techniques for the old art of relieving people of their money.

Cyberspace enables many new types of offence and novel ways of committing old offences, such as terrorism, piracy, fraud, identity theft, stalking, sexual offences against children, hacking security codes, racist harassment. The increased speed and extent of travel and communications signified by globalisation facilitates a variety of crimes: trafficking in people, drugs, and arms, money laundering, and terrorism, for example.

Opportunities

Criminal opportunities can be expanded by a proliferation of targets (for example the spread of ownership of cars, televisions, videos, DVD players, home PCs, laptops, and most recently, mobile phones, iPods, and iPads, each in turn becoming the hottest items for theft). Many studies have charted surges in particular kinds of theft following the development of new 'must-have' consumer goods. For example, there was a very sharp rise in robberies of phones from early 2000 to early 2002 (whilst thefts of other goods remained roughly static), tracking the rapid rise in ownership of mobile phones.

Controls

One further ingredient is necessary before a crime can be committed – the absence of controls, formal and informal. A potential burglar, say, may be eager to find a property to burgle, perhaps to feed her children or a habit. Equipped with jemmy and know-how, she comes across a relatively secluded house, milk bottles curdling on the doorstep indicating absent owners, and she spies the flashing LCDs of tempting electronic equipment through the ground floor window. But her progress up the garden path may be arrested by the plod of a patrolling constable's feet, or the sound of a siren. Even in the likely event that the strong arm of the law is deployed elsewhere, one final intervention may hold her back. On the shelf she spots a Bible, and hears the still, small voice of her

Sunday School teacher, 'Thou shalt not steal', and she goes home for tea and reflection.

Changes in the efficacy of *formal* criminal justice controls will alter the attractions or possibility of crime. The 1990s drop in crime in the USA has been popularly attributed to harder or smarter or simply more policing. 'Crime is down, blame the police' boasted former NYPD Chief (now Cameron adviser) Bratton. Others give the credit to tougher punishment, claiming vindication for Michael Howard's 'prison works' slogan.

Both claims are vigorously disputed, and the evidence supporting them is dubious. The very fact that the decline in crime was universal throughout the Western world in the last fifteen years, despite substantial variations in policing and penal policies in different jurisdictions, calls the parochial assertions of Bratton, Howard and their ilk into question.

Informal social controls are also important in interpretations of crime trends. The thesis that informal social controls – family, school, socialisation, community and 'cultural capital' – are the fundamental basis of social order has a long pedigree. However, a major problem facing the common conservative argument that increasing 'permissiveness' lies behind rising crime is to explain why crime has fallen in recent times despite no reversal of cultural liberalisation.

Crime has complex and multiple causes, so no single-factor accounts (like the conservative control thesis) can withstand close examination. The analysis in terms of five necessary conditions of crime provides a variety of tools for explaining particular turning points. For example, the explosion of crime in the Thatcher years (confirmed both by police statistics and the British Crime Survey) was attributable above all to the pernicious social effects (rapidly rising inequality and social exclusion) of the introduction of neo-liberal economic policies.

The fall in crime since the mid-1990s is harder to explain, as it is difficult to see any attenuation of 'criminality' (the tendency of society to produce criminals). The Right's bête noir of 'permissiveness' continued unabated, as did the economic and social polarisation attributable to neo-liberal globalisation.

The most plausible account is that there was a huge expansion in the use and efficacy of technical crime prevention techniques, from CCTV to car and home security devices. These have held the lid down on a continuing underlying increase in 'criminality', the propensity of a society to generate crime pressures. The riots confirm this, showing dramatically what happens when the lid is temporarily lifted.

Smart and fair criminal justice may reduce crime, but at best this can only be a short-term, first aid response. Raymond Chandler diagnosed it well in *The Long Goodbye*: "Crime isn't a disease, it's a symptom. Cops are like a doctor that gives you aspirin for a brain tumour."

It is necessary not only to be tough on crime but on its underlying causes, which lie way beyond the ambit of cops, courts and corrections. We need radical surgery to reconstruct a fairer, more inclusive society, not just sweep away the symptoms. Social peace requires social justice.

12. What the Public Really Think

Professor Julian V Roberts

Politicians have been increasingly wary of what is often assumed to be essentially illiberal mainstream public opinion on law and order. But, according to Julian V Roberts, they would do well to understand the limits of opinion polling, to try to reflect better the full complexity of public views, and to lead the public rather than simply follow if we are to achieve lower levels of crime in our communities.

Like it or not, public opinion has always influenced penal policy in this and most other western democracies. The strength of the public's voice has varied over time, and on some rare occasions – the abolition of the death penalty being the obvious example -- politicians have deliberately ignored community opinion. More often, though, criminal policy has been crafted with a view to reassuring the public that crime is punished with severity – whether with respect to antisocial behaviour, sentencing or other areas of criminal justice. Courts too, appear to have been influenced by public opinion. Research by Mike Hough and others suggests that part of the explanation for the inexorably rising prison population over the past 15 years has been the sensitivity of the courts to public opinion.[1]

To what extent public opinion should determine or influence penal policy is a complex question but this much seems clear: a criminal justice system totally blind to, or, worse, at odds with public opinion would founder. There must be some interface and communication between the community and the justice system, or public confidence in justice will decline as will co-operation with the justice system and compliance with the law.

My view is that the most important function that polling and academic research can serve is not to extract specific policies from public views but rather to gauge the degree of fit between penal policy and practice and community opinion. This can lead to a reflection as to whether these policies and practices need modification. A second purpose of polling is to identify the policies to which the public object most strongly, or the elements of criminal justice about which the public is most misinformed. This insight can then guide attempts to improve public knowledge of the justice system, and ultimately public confidence.

The research record on criminal justice in this country is now very substantial; more is known about the views of the British public than any other population. The pace of polling has accelerated in recent years – further evidence of the importance of public opinion to politicians and policy makers. What then have we learned from the polls and academic research?

Polls reveal only part of the picture
My first lesson is that no portrait of public opinion can rest on polls alone. Polls undermine sound penal policy development when they measure public opinion by posing simple questions which generate punitive, top-of-the-head reactions. Some politicians then use these polls to advance their own populist agenda.

Understanding public attitudes to crime and justice requires careful surveys using representative samples of the public as well as different methods, including focus groups, key informant interviews and laboratory-based research. A good example of this concerns the death penalty. If you simply ask people to choose the appropriate penalty for murder, almost all will choose execution or life without parole.[2] But give the public actual cases to consider, and these sentences will attract little support.[3]

Misperceptions of crime and justice abound

Most polls measure attitudes to criminal justice, but there are important lessons from the research which has measured public knowledge of crime and justice trends. That work shows that significant majorities of the public:

- Overestimate crime rates and re-offending rates;
- Underestimate the severity of punishment trends such as the custody rate or the lengths of prison sentences;
- Have little familiarity with the range of non-custodial options;
- Know little about key features of criminal justice – for example few people are aware of the extent to which the community is involved in sentencing through lay magistrates.

These findings are important: they provide insight into the evidence base on which the public relies when expressing opinions about criminal justice.[4] They also demonstrate why we cannot simply adjust criminal justice policies to make them more consistent with public views; doing so would lead to ineffective and unjust policies.

Perceptions are slow to change

Perceptions of crime and justice change slowly, or not at all. Polls have repeatedly demonstrated that most people see crime rates as constantly rising – regardless of trends from the BCS or police statistics. Attitudes are similarly intransigent: earlier this year a poll found that approximately two-thirds of the public believed that sentencing was too lenient – almost exactly the same proportion who held this view in 15 years ago.[5] Since then of course, sentencing has become much harsher and the prison population has risen significantly (Hough et al., 2003). The lesson, then, is that attitudes are relatively impervious to changes in the criminal justice environment.

Penal impatience

Many people's first reaction to offenders is punitive: we all display what I would call penal impatience -- a punitive reaction which expects instant results. We want offenders punished and we expect punishment to produce desistance from crime and compliance with the law. In reality, re-offending is a more likely outcome than desistance, whatever the sentence. This penal impatience manifests itself in poll results which show strong support for 'get tough' crime policies. Yet give people a little time -- and a range of options -- and they show strong support for restorative justice, crime prevention and judicial discretion rather than punishment and mandatory sentences. Mandatory sentences of imprisonment are a good example of how we can misread the public mood. Simple polls suggest high levels of support for mandatory sentencing, yet when given more options and actual cases to consider people prefer to trust judges.

Mitigation offers another illustration of what I mean. Research for the Sentencing Advisory Panel in 2009 found strong public support for a range of mitigating factors. Take the question of remorse: it might be expected that the cynical public has little time for expressions of remorse – he's probably faking it! Yet we found significant public support for this factor at sentencing: almost two-thirds of our sample thought that the expression of remorse justified the imposition of a community order instead of custody in a serious case of assault.[6]

Public views are complex, even in trying times

A more recent example of the complexity of public views can be seen in the public's reaction to the rioters over the summer of 2011. People were understandably outraged by the scale and nature of the offending. However, four out of five respondents to a poll agreed that "the more secure and stable your life is, the less likely you are to smash windows" – suggesting some awareness that social environment played a role in the disturbances.[7] People were also more likely to agree than disagree with the statement that "dismissing the social, political and economic is to ignore the frustrations of a group that feels increasingly marginalised". Finally, although the public expected a tough response to the rioters, fully one-third viewed the four-year sentences for the offenders who used Facebook to encourage rioters as being too harsh.

Throwing the book at offenders fails to capture the complete picture of public opinion. Punishment is not enough.

Prevention often more popular than punishment

Polls and research carried out in cooler times reveal a similar pattern: strong public support for prevention rather than mere punishment. Throwing the book at offenders fails to capture the complete picture of public opinion. Punishment is not enough. The following findings from research in the field of crime prevention are illustrative (see Roberts and Hastings, 2011 for a review):

- Across countries and over time, the public consistently shows more support for non-punitive responses such as child development programs than for punitive interventions such as harsher sentencing or stricter parole;

- When asked to allocate funding to various criminal justice priorities and initiatives, the public consistently favor prevention over punishment;

- The public wants value for money, and believes crime prevention is a cost-effective way of reducing crime. Members of the public also indicate that they would be willing to support politicians who move in this direction.

Sentencing is complicated and confusing

Another lesson involves our expectations of the public. Most people tend to be critical of criminal justice – and in particular the sentencing process. But let's be realistic here, sentencing in England and Wales is complicated and most people learn about sentencing from news media coverage that runs from the merely incomplete to the woefully inaccurate. Even if media coverage is relatively accurate, sentencing is hard to explain to the public. A recent example is the release from prison (on home detention curfew) of a peer sentenced during the expenses scandal. He was released from prison after serving one quarter of the sentence. Now, I am not arguing against graduated release from prison, but good luck to anyone who wants to convince the public that release at such an early point in the sentence makes sense.

Information helps improve attitudes

Let's end this brief chapter on a positive note. Researchers in several countries have attempted to change public attitudes or improve public confidence by providing information about the system. The general research strategy in this field has been to provide some members of the public with information about a particular issue such as the death penalty, community sentencing, or parole – and then to measure attitudes to the issue in question. These peoples' attitudes are then compared to those held by the general public or by other participants who have not been provided with information. Here are a couple of examples.

The first involved a 'deliberative poll' carried out in England in which almost 300 people spent a weekend together, hearing lectures, receiving information on crime and punishment and being given opportunities to 'deliberate' on the issues. The idea was to see to what extent public views differed from their top-of-the-head opinions, and to see if any change was durable over time. Analysis of 'before and after' surveys – including a follow-up survey ten months after the event – showed significant and lasting change, at least on some issues.[8] More recently, Mitchell and Roberts (2011) explored the role of knowledge in shaping public attitudes to sentencing for murder. Participants who were given information about sentencing were less critical of sentencing practices and less punitive in the sentences that they imposed in vignettes presented to them. Other studies which have demonstrated the effects of information on attitudes include: Singer and Cooper (2008); Salisbury (2004) and Chapman, Mirrlees-Black and Brawn (2002). The final lesson is therefore that attitudes can change, although it is never easy to achieve.

What should policy makers do with public opinion research? They should listen to the public but understand the limits of public knowledge. They should also attempt to reflect the complexity of public views, and not jump on the first policy proposal which seems likely to prove popular. Ultimately, there is also a role for politicians and policy makers to lead the public by informing them about principled and evidence based approaches to offending.

Footnotes

1 Hough, Jacobson and Millie 2003
2 Ipsos-MORI, 2007
3 For example, Mitchell and Roberts, 2011
4 See Roberts and Hough, 2005 for a review.
5 Hough and Roberts, 1998
6 Hough and Roberts, 2011
7 YouGov, 2011
8 See Hough and Park, 2002

References

Chapman, B., Mirrlees-Black, C. and Brawn, C. (2002) *Improving public attitudes to the Criminal Justice System: The impact of information*. HORS Number 245. London: Home Office.

Dawes, W., Harvey, P., McIntosh, B., Nunney, F. and Phillips, A. (2011) *Attitudes to Guilty Plea Sentence Reductions*. London: Sentencing Council of England and Wales.

Hough, M., Jacobson, J. and Millie, A. (2003) *The Decision to Imprison: Sentencing and the Prison Population.* London: Prison Reform Trust.

Hough, M. and Roberts, J.V. (1998) *Attitudes to punishment: findings from the BCS.* London:

Home Office.

Ipsos-MORI (2007) *Attitudes to the death penalty.* London: Ipsos-MORI.

Ipsos-MORI (2010) *Where are the public on crime and punishment?* London: Ipsos-MORI.

Roberts, J.V. and Hough, M. (2005) *Understanding Public Attitudes to Criminal Justice.* Maidenhead: Open University Press

Mitchell, B. and Roberts, J.V. (2011) Public Attitudes Towards the Mandatory Life Sentence for Murder in England and Wales. *Criminal Law Review*, 6: 456-465.

Roberts, J.V. and Hough, M. (2005) *Understanding Public Attitudes to Criminal Justice.* Maidenhead: Open University Press

Roberts, J.V. (2011) Community Views of Sentencing: Intuitive and Principled Responses to Offending. In: M. Tonry (ed.) *Punishment Futures.* Oxford: Oxford University Press.

Roberts, J.V. and Hough, M. (2011) Custody or Community? Exploring the Boundaries of Public Punitiveness in England and Wales. *Criminology and Criminal Justice*, 11: 185-202.

Singer, L. And Cooper, S. (2008) *Inform, persuade and remind. An evaluation of a project to improve public confidence in the criminal justice system.* London: Ministry of Justice.

YouGov poll, August 17/18, 2011.

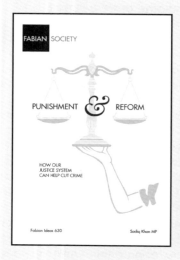

Discussion Guide: Punishment and Reform

How to use this Discussion Guide

The guide can be used in various ways by Fabian Local Societies, local political party meetings and trade union branches, student societies, NGOs and other groups.

■ You might hold a discussion among local members or invite a guest speaker – for example, an MP, academic or local practitioner to lead a group discussion.

■ Some different key themes are suggested. You might choose to spend 15 – 20 minutes on each area, or decide to focus the whole discussion on one of the issues for a more detailed discussion.

A discussion could address some or all of the following questions:

● What are the main causes of crime in our society? Should policy always be a mix of 'tough on crime, tough on the causes of crime', or are there exceptions?

● Public opinion is crucial in these debates – justice requires consent and if politicians do not bring the public with them there is understandable discontent. What do you think the balance should be between political leadership and simply following opinion polls? What do you think the public really believe?

● There is often a lot of talk about giving victims a greater role in the justice system. Are there practical ways to make this a reality? How appropriate is it anyway? What would the benefits and the dangers be?

● Our prison system has some deeply engrained problems. What are prisons really for? Where should progressive politicians place themselves in the balance between punishment and rehabilitation? What immediate steps could be taken to ensure that prisons work better?

Please let us know what you think

Whatever view you take of the issues, we would very much like to hear about your discussion. Please send us a summary of your debate (perhaps 300 words) to debate@fabians.org.uk.

The Solidarity Society

Why we can afford to end poverty, and how to do it with public support.

Tim Horton and James Gregory

This report sets out a strategy for how to reduce, eliminate and prevent poverty in Britain.

'The Solidarity Society' is the final report of a project to commemorate the centenary of Beatrice Webb's 1909 Minority Report of the Royal Commission on the Poor Law. It addresses how the values and insights of the Minority Report can animate and inspire a radical contemporary vision to fight and prevent poverty in modern Britain.

The report makes immediate proposals to help build momentum for deeper change. It also seeks to learn lessons from the successes and failures of post-war welfare history, as well as from international evidence on poverty prevention.

Separate and Unequal

How integration can deliver the good society

Nick Johnson

Britain is separate because it is unequal, and it is unequal because it is separate.

The gap between rich and poor, having exploded during the 1980s, is still growing, despite measures to address poverty in the 13 years of Labour Government. At the same time, we face growing fragmentation in our communities.

In this Fabian Ideas pamphlet, Nick Johnson argues that the politics of integration and equality have become fractured and that we can make the clearest case for both by showing what integration really means.

The effect that a more integrated society would have on all our lives will be a powerful message for progressive politicians: equality and integration must live together or fall apart.

JOIN THE FABIANS TODAY

Join us and receive at least four pamphlets or books a year as well as our quarterly magazine, 'Fabian Review'.

I'd like to become a Fabian for just £1 a month

I understand that should I wish to cancel at any time during my six-month introductory membership period, I will receive a refund and keep all publications received without obligation. After six months I understand my membership will revert to the monthly rate as published in *Fabian Review*, currently £3 (ordinary) or £1.50 (unwaged) by Direct Debit.

Name	Date of birth
Address	
	Postcode
Email	
Telephone	

Instruction to Bank   Originator's ID: 971666

Bank/building society name	
Address	
	Postcode
Acct holder(s)	
Acct no.	Sort code

I instruct you to pay direct debits from my account at the request of the Fabian Society. The instruction is subject to the safeguards of the Direct Debit Guarantee.

Signature	Date

Return to:
Fabian Society Membership
FREEPOST SW 1570
11 Dartmouth Street, London SW1H 9BN